BACKYARD
ROUGHING IT EASY

BACKYARD ROUGHING IT EASY

Dian Thomas

FAWCETT COLUMBINE ● NEW YORK

BACKYARD ROUGHING IT EASY

Copyright © 1980 Dian Thomas

Published by Fawcett Columbine Books, a unit of CBS Publications, the Consumer Publishing Division of CBS Inc.

ISBN: 0-449-90018-5

Printed in the United States of America

First Fawcett Columbine printing: June 1980

10 9 8 7 6 5 4 3 2 1

To my mother, Norene Richins Thomas,
whose creativity is limitless.

Contents

Introduction

There is a soothing quality in the outdoors that somehow both calms you down and lifts you up. It's hard to place your finger on exactly what the feeling is, but hundreds of thousands of people each year head for the national parks or other wilderness areas. They like to keep in touch with the out-of-doors, and hope to find that indefinable calm it brings.

Now, with money tight and gas not as available as it has been in the past, a lot of outdoor enthusiasts are despairing. They don't want to be cut off from those rewarding experiences, but they can't get to the camping country easily or as often as they once could.

Fortunately, you don't need to travel to enjoy outdoor experiences. You need only look as far as your backyard or patio or balcony. And you don't need to spend a lot of money, either. This book will show you how to improvise equipment from ordinary household items and how to enjoy your backyard in a new light. So, invite a few friends over, whip up some tasty food, and you're all set to enjoy the fun of the outdoors—without leaving home.

One chapter shows you how to use your wheelborrow as a barbecue, rotisserie, and briquet-cooking area. When you're finished, just wheel the wheelbarrow back into the garage. Or you can convert your old flowerpots into small hibachis for an unusual party. Or set up the ironing board for a backyard buffet, and iron your burritos and miniature pizzas in pocket bread. It's even faster than pressing Dad's shirt! (A great treat when you're pressed for time.)

Another chapter offers pointers on how to get the charcoal burning (it's not as hard as some people make it), and some unusual ways to use briquets. You can even use your portable hair dryer to get the coals glowing and ready to cook that thick, juicy steak.

Details on stick cooking, spit cooking, grill cooking, and foil cooking in other chapters will give you some new ideas on how to make cooking easy but fun in the out-of-doors. For example, you can cook an apple on a stick, dip it in sugar and cinnamon, then glaze it over by the coals, for a delicious dessert reminiscent of Grandma's apple pie. Or you can prepare foil dinners that are gourmet delights. There are even some tricks for grilling perfect steaks.

Some fun ideas for getting to know your family better are also included in another chapter, complete with "family activity night" suggestions to get the entire family involved. Try a "This Is Your Life!" night for a family member, or even a backwards dinner, or a tape-recorder scavenger hunt in which you hunt for sounds. You can have a great time, but most important, you become closer to your family and cement bonds of friendship that will keep your family together for a long time.

Unusual parties? An entire chapter is devoted to looking at some novel ideas for entertaining, including a flowerpot party, a garden party, and a party to cook a pig in your backyard.

So saddle up your enthusiasm for an adventure right outside your back door, and take off into the adventures that will fulfill your penchant for outdoor fun and spark your creativity, too.

I. Equipment

When your mind starts conjuring up the tantalizing aroma of juicy steaks, or a chicken browning on a spit, or succulent ribs, its time to treat barbecuing as serious business. The first step—finding the place to barbecue—is usually no problem. Most people have access to an appropriate barbecuing site, whether it's a backyard, a porch, a balcony, a local park, or your neighbor's patio.

Next, you will want to take stock of the barbecuing equipment you have, and what you will need. Some of it you may have to purchase; other equipment can easily be improvised with a little creativity and practically no expenditure of money. You can begin gathering appropriate cooking and serving equipment, with some basic tools that you might already have.

Some outdoor tools you will soon find a necessity:

- Long-handled fork, spoon, tongs, and spatula for turning and stirring the food without getting burned.
- Skewers for shish kebabs, marshmallows, apples, and other foods cooked on a stick.
- A good sharp carving knife and a portable carving board.
- Tongs, preferably long-handled, for arranging coals and turning meat and other food. By using tongs rather than a fork to turn meat, you avoid puncturing it, and thus preserve the juices.
- Meat thermometer for cooking large pieces of meat.
- Asbestos mitt or potholder to save your hands from hot metal or rocks.

Basic tools handy for backyard cooking.

- Heavy-duty aluminum foil.
- Long-handled basting brush or a new paint brush (1½" to 2 inches wide) for basting food and applying barbecue sauce. Be sure to wash well in warm soapy water after using for cooking. (If you use a paint brush, mark it so you won't use it for painting.)
- Seasonings, salt, pepper, and whatever else suits your taste to spice up your cooking.
- Mist bottle or water gun for dousing flames.
- Stiff metal brush for cleaning the grill after use.

Organizing Equipment

Now that you have gathered your cooking accessories, try to keep them together to help keep your outdoor fun hassle-free. (No more hunting and gathering each time you want to cook outdoors.) There are several ways to store your tools and keep them readily accessible.

Hanging Equipment Bag

Purchase a hanging shoebag with see-through pockets at a variety or department store. Sew down one side of all the pockets. On the pockets where small items such as utensils are to be stored sew up two inches on the opposite side to make sure items don't fall out. Store paper plates, napkins, eating utensils, and cups on one side, cooking utensils on the other. Long-handled equipment with leather loops can be hung over a coat hanger. This storage bag is handy to hang in a kitchen closet or utility closet, and easy to transfer to a branch or hook when you're cooking outdoors. If the weather turns bad, you can pack up in a jiffy, and all your cooking and eating utensils are well protected.

Hanging equipment bag.

Lunch box for
arranging small items.

Pop-bottle container as
equipment organizer.

Lunch Box

A lunch box makes an excellent storage box for small
items. The rounded thermos area is good for holding a
pancake turner, sharp knives, and other utensils. Before
putting the utensils in the box, cut a piece of cardboard and
tape it to the wires on the lunch box to hold the utensils in.
You can also store barbecue sauce in the thermos. Use the
sandwich area to store spices, utensils, and other such
items.

Pop-Bottle Container

The cardboard carrying cases for soft drinks are quite
sturdy, with natural compartments for storage, and they
take up little room. Keep spices, utensils, hot pads, and
other handy items in the various compartments. Cardboard
mailing tubes or map holders can be used to hold some of
the long-handled utensils.

Plastic Cleaning Container

Similar in shape to the pop-bottle container, but sturdier and more durable, these can be purchased in most houseware departments. Organize utensils and spices in the various compartments.

Tackle Box

A small tackle box can also be made into a container for equipment in the backyard. Spatulas, knives, peelers, etc., can be placed in the bottom, and seasonings can be placed in the trays. The tackle boxes come in different sizes, so look for a tackle box that will fit your needs. Place it near your grill so it is handy to use each time.

Carpenter's Apron

If you want all of your spices and tools at your fingertips, you may simply wish to purchase a carpenter's apron and fill it up with your cooking necessities.

Carpenter's apron for keeping equipment handy.

Towel
barbeque apron.

Towel Barbecue Apron

A handy barbecue apron can be made from a large bath towel, one yard of T-shirt ribbing, and two yards of ribbon or bias binding. To begin your apron, fold the towel horizontally about eight inches from one end and cut a crescent-shaped wedge (about four inches deep at the center and as wide as half the circumference of your head) along the fold for your head. The neck hole should form a horizontal football shape on the towel. Sew the T-shirt ribbing around the neck opening. Next sew ribbon or bias binding to bottom end of the towel, then turn up ten inches and stitch along each side to form a pocket. Stitch vertically at intervals for individual pockets to hold spices, cooking tools, and hot pads. To make your apron fancier, embroider or add appliques.

Picnic Basket

A used bushel basket makes a good-looking picnic basket once it is lined.

Materials needed:

2½ yards of 45-inch wide
    fabric, 1¾ yards print and
    ¾ yard solid
1½ yards ½-inch wide elastic
3 yards ball fringe or other
    trim for lid (optional)
4 feet cord for handles, cut
    in 2-24 in. pieces
1 can spray paint (desired
    color) or varnish
1 package bias tape (optional)
2 washers (optional)
1 bushel basket

Out of newsprint, cut the following pattern pieces:

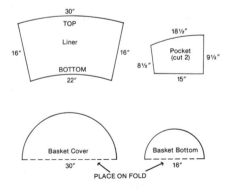

Pattern pieces.   Looking into picnic basket.

Place the pattern on material that has been doubled, or folded. Cover and bottom pieces should go on the fold to make complete circle. Cut out pieces. Sew two liner pieces together to make a ring. Sew two pocket pieces together. Hem top of pockets or trim with bias tape. Pin in place on basket liner, and sew side seams of basket line and pockets together. Sew seams through pockets onto liner to make several different sized pockets. Pin liner and pockets to the basket bottom, right sides together (may need to gather or pleat). Stitch. Make a casing in the top of liner and insert elastic.

Basket Cover: Sew on ball fringe or trim. Measure and sew elastic (52 inches approximately) three inches from the edge. Drill holes in basket on both sides and run cord through for handles. Tie knots on end of cord inside basket. To make handle holes more secure, use washers.

Commercial Grills

A variety of commercial grills are available for the would-be outdoor chef. (If you are strapped by a tight budget, or not sure how committed you are to outdoor cooking, you may want to use an improvised grill, explained in the next section of this chapter.) With a little reading, you should be able to find the grill that precisely suits your needs.

Hibachi

The advantage of these small grills is their portability. You can grill on your patio, at the beach, or in the woods. Hibachis come in various sizes, suitable for cooking hors d'oeuvres, kebabs, hamburgers, and steaks. Most are made of cast iron. Meals cooked on a hibachi are limited to a few people, due to the small grill size.

Open Brazier

Excellent for cooking flat pieces of meat, such as hamburgers, fish, chicken pieces, and steaks. The open brazier consists of a grill over a shallow fire bowl set on three or four legs. It is the most popular type of commercial grill, and can be found in several sizes. An open brazier is usually lightweight and has wheels for easy moving. Look for one that allows you to move the grill up and down to regulate the heat.

Hibachi grill.

Open brazier.   Commercial kettle cooker.

Cooking Kettle

Convenient for cooking large pieces of food, a covered kettle is like a huge Dutch oven on wheels. Dampers on the bottom and the top can be opened to raise the temperature or closed to lower it. Cooking with the lid on creates an oven effect.

Gas Grill

Gas barbecues eliminate the need to build a fire, as well as the need to clean up after you have finished cooking. They have the advantage of easily controllable and consistent heat. Some units use bottled gas, others use natural gas. The gas is used to heat a layer of volcanic or ceramic rocks, which in turn radiate heat to the food. Since you don't need to wait for coals to burn down, you can start

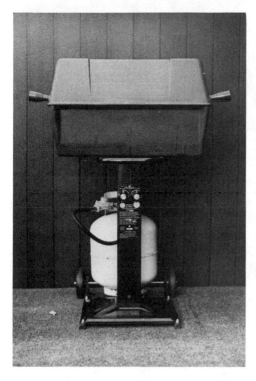

Commercial gas grill.   Commercial smoke cooker.

barbecuing only a few minutes after the grill has been turned on. These units are usually more expensive than other grills, but the cost may even out if the grill is used frequently.

Smoke Cooker

Smoke ovens offer a good way to cook large cuts of meat slowly. There are many variations of smoke ovens. Japanese *kamodos,* for instance, are barrel-shaped barbecues with domed lids made of heavy ceramic or metal. Charcoal briquets in a fire bowl at the base of the oven provide heat. Once the briquets are started, sprinkle your favorite wood shavings over the charcoal to provide an aromatic smoke that slowly cooks the meat suspended on a grill or from a hook. If you are adventurous, you may want to try sprinkling your favorite herbs over the charcoal.

Another variation, the charcoal-water cooker, includes a container of water suspended on a grill above the fire pan and below the meat. The steam from the water helps to cook the meat, leaving it juicy and tender. The advantage to this kind of cooker is that once set up, food can be left to cook without tending for a long period of time.

Improvised Grills

Adventurous cooks will want to try making their own grills. A good backyard grill can be made from a child's wagon or a garbage-can lid. The following should give you some ideas.

Wheelbarrow grill set up for rotisserie, grill and open-coals cooking.

Wheelborrow Grill

You can make a versatile barbecue that will handle a whole meal by using a wheelbarrow, a few bricks, some foil, and dirt. The great advantage of this grill is that you can wheel it wherever you want, and it is just the right height for you to sit on a lawn chair to roast apples, hot dogs, or marshmallows on a stick. The wheelbarrow provides enough space for a rotisserie and a grill, as well as for direct cooking on the coals.

Fill the wheelbarrow with gravel, sand, or dirt about six inches deep (enough to insulate it from the heat). For efficient briquet cooking, cover the area where the briquets will be placed with extra-heavy aluminum foil. The foil keeps the briquets from nestling into the sand or dirt and insures that air will circulate to keep the briquets burning. Stack the briquets in the center of the wheelbarrow and light them. When they are hot, spread them over the foil (see chapter 2).

Once the briquets are burning, line the sides of the wheelbarrow with bricks, then place a large grill across them for barbecuing flat pieces of meat. (For easy cleaning, spray the rack with nonstick cooking spray before using it.) You can regulate the cooking temperature by adding or taking away bricks to raise or lower your grill. Increase the heat by using fewer bricks, decrease it by adding more. The most efficient grill height is about four to six inches above the coals. If you simply want to use the coals for stick cooking, you needn't bother with the bricks or rack.

You can also try one of the following alternative arrangements:

- Rotisserie, grill, and open coals—use bricks on the back for a rotisserie, bricks just in front to support a wire rack, and then leave an open space for cooking over open coals.
- Rotisserie and open grill—stack bricks at the back for a rotisserie, and bricks along the side with a rack on them for a grill.
- Grill—Place bricks in four corners and put rack on top.

- Open coals—Cook directly on or over coals, using foil or stick cooking methods.

A couple of cautions and one helpful hint: Don't use refrigerator racks as grills. Some contain a harmful substance that is released by the heat. Cover the wheelbarrow after briquets are out so the dirt doesn't get wet from rain or dew. Moisture will tend to rust out the bottom of the wheelbarrow. (If you keep it covered with heavy plastic when not in use, one load of dirt should last the entire summer.) Slide a pair of mitt-type pot holders onto the handles of the wheelbarrow so that they will be handy while you are grilling.

Child's Wagon Grill

Fill with dirt and follow basic directions given for Wheelbarrow Grill.

Wagon grill.

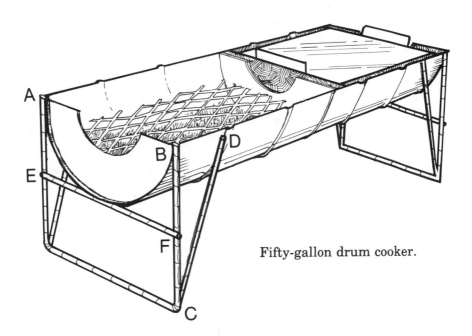

A B C D E F

Fifty-gallon drum cooker.

Fifty-Gallon Drum Cooker

To make a large grill that doesn't cost much, you might consider this project. All you will need to construct your grill is one fifty-gallon drum, two 84-inch-long pieces of ½-inch re-bar, steel reinforcement rod, four 30-inch pieces of ⅜-inch re-bar two 22-inch-long pieces of ⅜-inch re-bar, racks or heavy wire mesh, and some bricks.

Find a used fifty-gallon drum at a service station, junk dealer, or salvage yard. Make sure that it still has both ends in it. You will need to clean it out well, especially if it contained a petroleum product. A good way to clean it out is to go to a car wash, open both holes in the end of the drum, drain out any residue in the drum, and place it on its side with the large hole at the top and the small hole at the bottom. Place the washer wand in the large hole, then turn on the hot, soapy water and wash out the drum thoroughly. Let it drain completely. If you smell anything besides soap in the drum, repeat the soaping process until the drum is absolutely clean. (If *any* petroleum product is left in the drum, it might cause an explosion when it is cut in two.)

Next, you will need to cut the drum in half. Make a chalk mark *lengthwise* around the drum, measuring to make sure that the line cuts the drum exactly in half. Then use an acetylene torch to cut the drum, or pay a welder or school shop class to do it for you. Mark and cut out a 12-inch-diameter half-circle from each end of the barrel (as shown in illustration) for air flow and for adding fuel. After the metal has cooled, file and smooth the rough edges.

For legs, use two pieces of ½-inch re-bar 84 inches long. Measure 30 inches from each end of each piece and bend to form a right angle. (Using the torch to heat the part you bend will make bending the metal much easier.) Weld re-bar legs to points A and B on the illustration. Then using four pieces of ⅜-inch re-bar 30 inches long, weld at points C and D to brace the legs at the ends of the barbecue. Two crossmember pieces of ⅜-inch re-bar 22 inches long are welded at points E and F for extra lateral support.

From a metal supply house or salvage yard, buy a piece of heavy wire mesh 18″ x 34″. Place the mesh on two bricks inside the drum to hold your charcoal briquets, before you add the grill. Again, by adding or subtracting bricks, you can place the grill as close or as far from the charcoal as you like.

If you are not going to be moving the grill from place to place, instead of using bricks, fill the drum partially with sand, gravel or dirt. Place a piece of heavy-duty aluminum foil over the filling, and put the briquets on the foil. Remember that about four inches above the coals is a good height for the cooking rack.

Garbage-Can Lid

Another type of improvised grill can be made with a metal garbage can lid or almost any metal container that can hold dirt for insulation. The lid can be turned over to rest on three bricks, and is then filled with dirt. Cover dirt with extra heavy-duty foil and place briquets in a pile. The briquets can then be lit, bricks placed along the sides, and a grill placed on top of the bricks. Even a five-gallon nongalvanized can or bucket can be filled with dirt to about six inches from the top of the container and used. (A small vent should be cut about the height of the briquets in the five-gallon can to increase the flow of oxygen across the briquets.)

Whatever kind of metal container you use, be sure to leave about four to six inches between the meat and charcoal briquets. Keep in mind that cookie cooling racks can also be used as grills.

Garbage-can lid set up as a grill.

Grill made from bricks, foil, and a rack.

Bricks and Cinder Blocks

On a beautiful summer evening, you can cook a delicious outdoor meal simply by building a barbecue using bricks or cinder blocks, a grill, charcoal briquets, and aluminum foil. Put the bricks directly on the ground to support the rack used for grilling the meat. Place foil on the ground, arrange briquets on the foil; then light. Use a cookie cooling rack or an oven rack to cook on.

Campfire Rack

Easily set up on an open dirt area, a campfire rack works very well for a backyard barbecue. Campfire racks can usually be purchased at sporting-goods stores. Coals are placed on the ground and the campfire rack is set six to eight inches above them. If the dirt is loose or sandy, place a piece of heavy foil over it to keep the briquets from settling into the sand, which would cut off the heat, as well as the oxygen.

The campfire rack is ideal for regulating heat. To increase the intensity of the heat, you simply push the rack into the ground. To lower the heat, you pull the rack up.

Flowerpot

Ideal for cooking on the balcony of an apartment, the earthenware flowerpot grill is portable and easily stored. Have a flowerpot party and ask each couple to bring their own flowerpot and rack.

Use a pot at least eleven inches high and eleven inches in diameter. (Be sure to use a nonglazed pot.) Fill with dirt or gravel to within five to six inches of the top. Cover the dirt or gravel with foil so that the briquets will have better ventilation. Pile the briquets on the foil, light them, and place the rack on top of the pot. When the coals are ready, cook the meat. If the coals get too hot, remove the rack (with the meat on it), and sprinkle the briquets with water, or spray them lightly with a spray bottle filled with water to cool them down. It is best to remove the meat while you spray so that flying ash doesn't land on it. You can use the flowerpot for grill cooking, stick cooking, or direct-coal cooking.

Flowerpot grill showing dirt, foil, briquets, and grill rack.

Flowerpot grill.

Rolling a
newspaper
"log."

Five-Gallon Newspaper Stove

For low-cost fuel and a quick way to grill hamburgers, a newspaper stove is a good alternative to standard grills. All you need to make one is a five-gallon can, a wire cooling rack, some newspaper, and a spray bottle of water.

To make the grill, remove the top from the five-gallon can. Cut a 2½ inch by 1½ inch vent on one side of the can, about two inches from the bottom. Remove all pages with color printing, as they contain a toxic substance. Use about five or six pages of newspaper. Holding the section of paper with both hands, gradually gather the paper together, then twist to form small "logs" to place in the stove bottom. Repeat this procedure about four times, or until the can is half filled. Then wad up a single sheet of newspaper, set it on top of the "logs," and light.

Place the cooling rack over the top of the can as a grill. Meat that is not more than an inch thick, with some fat content, cooks well on this stove. The fat dripping down on the newspapers keeps them burning. If the flames burn too high, spray them with water to avoid charred, half-cooked food.

After you have cooked hamburgers or other meat on the newspaper stove, you can cook Hawaiian banana boats for dessert. Place the banana boats sealed in foil in the bottom of the can, wad up another five to six sheets of newspaper on top of them, and light the paper. Replace the greasy cooling rack on the top of the can, and the flames will burn the grease off the grill and warm the banana boats at the same time. After the newspapers have burned down, remove the rack, take out the banana boats, and enjoy. When the rack is cool, clean it with a pad of fine steel wool and then a damp cloth.

Vertical Spit

For an unusual way of cooking a chicken—or even a turkey—outdoors, you might want to try a vertical spit. It works like an outdoor oven; the meat slowly cooks in the pocket of heat created by the vertically placed coals. The equipment needed for the vertical spit includes: four three-foot-long metal stakes; a tripod, which can be made by tying together three straight sticks or pieces of five-foot-long metal tubing; chicken wire; aluminum foil; and charcoal briquets.

First, drive the four metal stakes into the ground to form a square. The distance between stakes depends on the meat you are cooking. For instance, stakes should be 12 to 14 inches apart for chickens, and 24 to 28 inches apart for turkeys. Then cut four pieces of one-inch mesh chicken wire about two feet long and ten holes wide (cut down the center of the eleventh hole). Fasten the long sides of each roll together to make four long tubelike wire cages. Slip each wire cage over a metal stake and fill each cage with charcoal briquets. You can use briquets that have been presoaked to facilitate lighting. Be sure not to add any more starter fluid once the fire is lit because this could cause an explosion in the starter can as the flame is sucked into the can.

After the briquets are hot, wrap aluminum foil—shiny side in—around the outside of the four stakes to hold the heat in the enclosed area. You will need to add a few briquets to the wire cages every half hour to maintain a constant temperature. Plan on using about ten to fifteen pounds of briquets. Center the tripod over the four stakes.

Prepare the poultry as if you were cooking it in the oven. To keep the wings from overcooking, tie them close to the body with a piece of heavy string. Slip an oven brown-in bag around the bird to protect it from briquet ashes and to retain juices. Then tie a piece of heavy string or light-weight wire around the legs of the bird. Use a piece long enough so that the bird will dangle a few inches above the ground when tied to the top of the tripod. It should take about 1½ hours to roast a chicken, but it depends on the size of your bird and the temperature you are able to maintain.

Hang an inexpensive oven thermometer by a wire from the tripod at the same level as the bird to help determine the temperature inside the vertical spit. The temperature should be about 350 degrees F. If the temperature inside the foil square becomes too hot, slide the foil several inches up from the ground or open the foil to allow more circula-tion of air and thus lower the temperature. If the tempera-ture is lower than 350 degrees F., cook the bird longer. Be sure the temperature does not go below 300 degrees F. if the bird is stuffed, to avoid food poisoning. For barbecued chicken, baste the poultry before cooking, or slip the oven bag off the bird about fifteen minutes before it is done and baste it with your favorite barbecue sauce. If the chicken browns too much, wrap it in foil to stop the browning; it will continue to cook but won't brown.

Cooking with a vertical spit.

Filling wire cages with
charcoal briquets.

Hooking bird to tripod.

Creative Accessories for Parties

You needn't be handicapped at party time if you don't have all the equipment you need. There are all sorts of improvisations you can come up with to make your party a successful one that your guests will remember for a long time. These handy items will make cooking more convenient and more fun.

Shovel Frying Pan

You can transform a shovel into a frying pan or solid grill for cooking eggs or meats. Clean a heavy shovel, then cover the top of the shovel with extra-heavy-duty aluminum foil (or two to three layers of regular foil). Use the shovel frypan by setting it directly on the coals or by propping it on rocks or bricks above the coals.

Shovel frying pan.   Pitchfork skewers.

Grilling food, using a cooking shirt.

Pitchfork Skewers

For variety, use a new or well-cleaned pitchfork as a multiple skewer for hot dogs, marshmallows, or shish kebabs. To sterilize a well-cleaned pitchfork, place it directly on the hot fire for several minutes, cool it, wipe it off, and it is ready to use. You may even wish to purchase one just for the novelty.

Cooking Shirt

To help you handle hot dishes or grills when there is no potholder around, a cooking shirt is especially convenient. It can double as an apron, too.

Simply choose an old long-sleeved shirt or a shirt you don't mind cutting up, and cut off the sleeves at about elbow

Using a handy soap-bottle cleaner.

length. Then cut off the sleeves of a long-sleeved sweatshirt at shoulder level. Slip the sweatshirt sleeve up the inside of the regular shirt sleeve until the width of the sweatshirt sleeve corresponds to the width of the shirt sleeve you will be sewing it to. Then sew the long sweatshirt sleeve to the shirt sleeve, forming an inside seam. You now have adjustable potholders at the tips of your fingers, simply by pulling down the sweatshirt sleeves and lapping them over your hands. You can push the sweatshirt sleeves up above your wrists until you want to handle something hot again.

Soap Bottle Cleaner

When you are in the backyard and need to wash your hands, but don't want to keep running back and forth into the house, an empty liquid soap squirt bottle provides a happy solution. Fill it with water, add a dash of dish detergent, then squeeze the solution out as needed for cleaning messy hands.

Serving Accessories

Using creativity in the way you serve enhances what you serve. These ideas also help you serve food efficiently, avoiding meal-time hassle.

Ironing-Board Buffet

Don't restrict yourself to using an ironing board solely for ironing—it can also be used as a portable buffet or table for equipment when barbecuing. A picnic cloth or oilcloth is excellent for covering the board. To organize the buffet, use the ironing board to hold paper plates, cups, and napkins, or arrange your food on it. Just be sure to place the ironing board on a solid, level surface, and check to make sure it is secure before placing objects on it. Secure the legs with bags filled with sand or dirt or place bricks to make the ironing board more stable. (See Chapter 7 for the Laundry Party.)

Ironing-board buffet.

Salad Bar and Pop Station

For creative serving use a laundry basket, a wheelbarrow, a plastic baby tub, or even a large garbage bag. For a large party use a child's wading pool. Line the container with plastic, then fill it with crushed ice. If you need to keep the food cold over a long period of time, nestle wrapped dry ice in the crushed ice. Place soda cans in the ice around the outer edges of the container. Then place salad bowls and dishes with dressings in the middle of the container. The most secure way to place the bowl is to make an indentation in the ice with your hand, place the bowl in the indentation, then twist it from side to side. For an inventive salad variation, make a fruit salad in a scooped-out watermelon half or place a cabbage head on the ice, then insert hors d'oeuvres on toothpicks into the head. Stick olives, cheese, shrimp, ham, radishes, pickles, vienna sausages, orange slices, and other tasty tidbits on the toothpicks.

Laundry-basket salad
bar and soda station.

Ice bowl.

Ice Bowl

If you need to keep food cold for a long period of time, instead of using ice cubes, purchase blocks of ice. Place the ice on a large tray or pan that will hold water and can be emptied periodically or directly on the ground. Chip out hollows on top of the ice just slightly smaller than the bowls that will contain the salad, fruit, and other things that you wish to keep cold. Then using metal bowls that can take extreme heat, fill the bowls with hot water—before the food is in them—and slide them around in the hollows on top of the ice until each hollow fits the bottom of its bowl. You may need to change the hot water in the bowls more than once. Once the food is in the bowls this solid ice counter will chill the bowls, and keep salads and fruits cold for a long period of time.

Ice for Punch

Colorful ice rings in your outdoor punchbowl will not only keep your punch cool, but will add elegance to your party. Coordinate the ice ring with the theme, colors, or decorations of your party. For interest add maraschino cherries, pineapple, mandarin orange sections, berries, mint or other leaves, or small flowers to your ice ring, or create contrast by adding food coloring to the water you're freezing.

To make your ice ring, gather the fruit or other decorations you are going to use and an interestingly shaped pan—Bundt pans, jello molds, spring pans, or even plastic cups for smaller cubes make good ice molds. Arrange the fruit or decorations in the bottom of the pan, upside down, so that they will look natural when you turn the molded ice over, then pour a shallow layer of water into the pan. Use just enough to cover the decorations. Freeze for one to two hours until the water has frozen, setting decorations in place, then add the rest of the water and freeze. To have a multicolored fruit ring, tint the first layer one color, then add a different food color to each new layer. Make sure each layer is completely frozen before you add the next, however.

Some alternate kinds of party ice include freezing tiny decorations in regular ice cubes. Freezing fruit juices or the punch itself to form your ice ring or cubes adds flavor instead of diluting your punch as the ice melts. Whatever kind of ice you choose, you probably should freeze your ice ring a day or two before the party to cut down on party-day rush.

Double-Boiler Food Keeper

Place ice in the bottom of a double boiler, and then put food that you want to keep cool in the top pan. It is great for

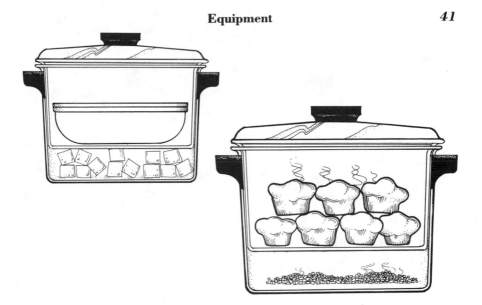

Double-boiler food keeper.

chilled salads. Cover the pan with a lid when you are not serving.

To keep foods warm while serving, place rock salt that has been heated in a metal dish or a pan over coals or in your oven in the bottom of the double boiler, then place the food you want to keep warm in the top and cover it with the lid. This works especially well if you want to fix the food before your guests arrive.

Frisbee Plate Holder

If you have ever dropped or leaked food because of a soggy paper plate, you will appreciate this new approach. Paper plates fit snugly into most frisbees. Frisbees support the plates when you cut food, and provide a sporty dash of color to your table. These holders come in handy when you are serving buffet style and people are eating without benefit of tables or trays.

Paper-bag lantern.

Paper-Bag Lantern

An easy and inexpensive way to light an outdoor eating area is to fill lunch-sized paper bags with an inch or two of sand. Set a votive candle in the middle of the sand in each bag, then light. Bag-lanterns make great lights for entry ways and patio parties.

Tablecloth Tips

An attractive picnic table complements any outdoor meal. These practical suggestions will beautify your table and help to solve any problems you are likely to encounter eating outdoors.

You can make picnic tablecloths from designer bedsheets, practical terry cloth, lightweight, washable Indian bedspreads, or from attractive oilcloths or denims.

Whether you buy a tablecloth or make your own, you will find that the breeze that cools your picnic will also blow your tablecloth into your food—and sometimes off the table. To avoid the battle of the breeze, try these tricks.

Windproof Table Cover

One creative way to beat the breeze is to make your own tablecloth with special pockets to hold each eater's utensils, napkins, and paper plates. Slipping the equipment in their pockets and anchoring paper cups by filling with ice cubes will keep your eating utensils on the table where you want them. One table cover has pockets shaped like half-slices of watermelon made from appliqued green, red, and black cotton fabric. Each half watermelon is stitched to divide the pocket into three smaller pockets, a large pocket for paper plate flanked by smaller ones to hold flatware and napkin.

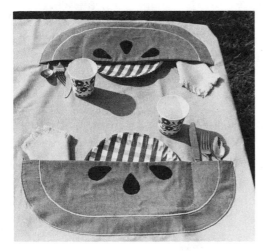

Table setting held securely against breezes in windproof table cover.

Sandbag Weights

Sew tiny two-inch-square sandbags from colorful scraps of cloth and fill with sand or pebbles. Attach each bag with yarn to a clothespin by threading the yarn through the clothespin's metal coil and then sewing the end of the yarn to the sandbag. Snap the clothespin-sandbags to the edges of your tablecloth on windy days.

Rod Weights

Another solution requires heavy dowels or round metal curtain rods (the kind that consist of one straight piece with no protruding ends). Sew a one-to-three-inch-wide hem—large enough to accommodate the dowel or rod you are using—along the two overhanging sides to your tablecloth, then slip in the rods or dowels to act as weights to hold the cloth in place. If you are making your own tablecloth, just cut the material two to four inches longer than you want the cloth to hang, then turn under the excess to form a pocket for the dowel or rod, as well as a hem for your cloth.

Drapery Weights

Sewing drapery weights into the hem of your tablecloths is another device. One clever person disguised the weights by covering them with flowerpot-shaped pockets to hold napkins. Appliquéd flowers stretch from the pot to "bloom" at the center of the tablecloth. The colorful "flowers" form pockets for securing paper plates against the wind. (The centers of the flowers conceal drapery weights as well.)

Insect Control

All too often flies, ants, wasps, mosquitoes, or other uninvited creatures feel they have a right to dine along with you—and sometimes on you. There are ways to discourage these bugs, but it takes a little planning.

Commercial Methods

One way to help prevent bugs from invading a party is to spray the yard thoroughly about forty-five minutes before the party with an outdoor insect spray. Forty-five minutes allows enough time for the bugs and spray to settle down before the party starts.

If you have an outdoor patio, pest strips hung in strategic but unobtrusive places can help cut down on bug problems. Also, treating plants that are particularly troubled with insects will help keep bugs away from the party. Another tip: Don't water your lawn the day of the party. Water always attracts bugs.

Lights

To add a decorative touch, you may want to use Christmas-tree lights to brighten an evening party. Colored lights, especially yellow ones, do not attract bugs as much as white lights do, so you are actually discouraging the insects while creating an atmosphere for a festive evening.

Embroidery-Hoop Lid

One easy solution to keeping flies off serving dishes before or during an outdoor feast is to use the embroidery-hoop technique. Simply tear off a piece of plastic wrap of suitable length and fasten it between the two embroidery hoops as if it were a piece of cloth to be embroidered. Place the hoops over plates and bowls and you will discourage the flies from joining you.

Net Tablecloth

Another way to keep insects from your food is to set the table and then cover it completely with colorful nylon netting until guests come to the table. Inexpensive netting is available up to 72 inches wide. Food looks pretty through the netting, and the netting is washable.

Fan

When you are working to prepare food for cooking, insects are especially unwelcome helpers. Set up your work table with two large fans facing each other and turned on high. This will not only help keep the insects off the food, but will make it much cooler for you to work. It will also keep the food cooler and fresher while you are preparing it.

2. Fire

Anyone who has spent much time around a campfire can tell you how exciting it is to sit and watch the embers glow. There is a hypnotizing magic about a fire as it dwindles into ashes. But if you can't get to the woods, having a cookout in your backyard will evoke some of that same feeling, especially when it is accompanied by delicious hot food.

A fire made from hardwood works well for cooking, but most people don't have the facilities to build one in the backyard, so the next best thing is to use charcoal briquets. These small pillow-shaped coals provide a steady, glowing heat suitable for outdoor cooking. They are made from wood and other combustible materials that have been burned, ground, mixed with a binder, and then compressed. Because the base material varies with the brand, they burn differently. Try two or three brands until you find the one you like best. Whatever brand of briquet you choose, the more you use it the better you will be able to control the heat and anticipate how long it will take to cook your food.

A few cautions about using briquets: Never use them indoors, because they emit carbon monoxide, a colorless, odorless gas that can kill, and never use gasoline to light briquets. Always use a charcoal starter or other method especially designed for this purpose.

The first step in getting ready for a backyard barbecue is to select the place the fire or charcoal will be lit. You'll want to barbecue on a level, open area at least six feet from flammable materials such as buildings, shrubs, dry grass, wood, or overhanging branches. If you are using a commercial barbecue with legs, however, it is not as critical to clear the area.

Preparing the Area

If you are going to start charcoal briquets on dirt, sand, or gravel, you may also want to put down a layer of heavy-duty aluminum foil first. Foil keeps the charcoals from becoming imbedded in the sand or dirt and helps to maintain the necessary air circulation. If you have a commercial barbecue, the charcoal-briquet fire can be built right in the bowl of the grill. Small hibachis have a grid that allows air to circulate underneath.

Starting Charcoal Briquets

Charcoal briquets that won't start can be a disaster at a party. Nothing can make a host feel more uneasy than hungry guests eager to eat sizzling steaks right off the grill who have to wait for twenty or thirty minutes for the charcoal to heat before the steaks can even be placed on the grill. Try to learn a sure method for starting briquets. The following list should help you find the one that works best for you.

Charcoal Starters

The most common method for starting charcoal briquets is to pile them into a pyramid and soak them with charcoal starter. Let the fluid-saturated briquets sit for three to four minutes before lighting. Then place a lighted match onto the charcoal briquets, which should start a flame burning over the briquets. After burning for approximately five to ten minutes, the fire will burn down, but the charcoal will continue to heat. You will know that the briquets are heating properly when white ash begins to form around the edges. Twenty to forty minutes are needed before the charcoal briquets are ready for cooking. The time depends on the type of briquets, the starter fluid, and the amount of wind. Don't add more starter fluid once the flame goes out, because if a flame is still in the briquets, the flame could flare up into the can and cause an explosion. Instead, be sure to douse the briquets thoroughly with starter fluid *before* you light them.

Electric Starters

A commercial electric starter can be purchased at most hardware stores. This is a circular metal device that is plugged into an electrical outlet. You place it in the center of a pyramid-shaped stack of briquets, and they begin heating. The briquets nearest the metal heat first.

Charcoal Marinating Cans

Although you can purchase commercially marinated briquets (soaked in a flammable substance to make them ignite quickly), they are expensive. If you do a lot of barbecuing, you may want to set up your own charcoal marinating can. Take a number 10 (one-gallon) can and fill it with charcoal briquets. Then pour starter fluid over them until they are covered. Let them stand overnight, or allow the briquets to stand in the "marinade" until they cease to bubble. At this point they are ready to use. When using marinated briquets, use a mixture of half-marinated and half-dry briquets, stacking them alternately in pyramid fashion, then light. Add more briquets to the "marinade" for your next barbecue. Add starter fluid to cover the briquets, then cover the can with a tight-fitting lid. Place the container in an area where it will not be a fire hazard.

If your picnic is not in your backyard, you may want to take just a few marinated briquets with you in a Ziploc bag. Wrap the bag in a piece of heavy-duty foil by placing the Ziploc bag in the center of the foil. Bring the sides of the foil up to the top so there is four inches overlapping them and fold down in small folds. Flatten on each side and

Briquets in can covered with fluid for marinating.

Marinated briquets in a Ziploc bag.

roll in to keep the briquets sealed off and to prevent the bag from being punctured. When you arrive at the area where you are going to build the barbecue fire, simply open up the foil, remove the briquets from the Ziploc bag, place them on the foil, and light.

Wire Basket

If you are using an open fire, the best way to start the charcoal briquets is to place them in a wire basket, which you can make out of heavy wire. Then put the basket into the flames. Briquets will light very quickly this way.

Chimney can.

Chimney Can

You can turn a number 10 can into a "chimney can" that will start charcoal briquets with the help of newspapers. Take a number 10 (one-gallon) can, cut out the top and bottom, poke holes around the can near the bottom with a punch-type can opener, and place it on the ground. Wad up several newspapers and place them in the can. Then pile briquets on top of the newspapers, about halfway to the top of the can. Place a rock underneath one edge of the can to provide a draft area, then light the papers. Once the briquets start burning, add more briquets from the top. The hot briquets should ignite the new briquets. If you have problems, fan a paper plate at the bottom where you have propped up the can to help air circulate enough to fire up the charcoal briquets. Once the charcoal briquets are lit, you can lift the can away from them with a pair of pliers and the briquets will spread out, ready for cooking. This method is very successful with marinated briquets.

Speeding Up the Briquets

If you find your briquets are not ready for cooking, speed up the heating process by carefully using one of these following methods:

- Hair blower. A portable hair blower is one of the best ways of speeding up charcoal briquets. The hot air is forced across the briquets, causing them to glow with a light flame, spreading the heat throughout the briquets almost instantly. Briquets can be heated in about ten or fifteen minutes using this method. Caution: Keep molded plastic hair blowers away from the intense heat of the briquets.
- Vacuum cleaner. If you have a small vacuum that blows from the back, hold it over the briquets. This method works in the same way as a hair blower.
- Fan. A small fan can also be used if it is safe to set near the briquets. (Be sure little children can't get to it.)
- Bellows. A fireplace bellows can be used to speed the heating process.
- Fan with plate. If you do not have access to any of these other methods, just fan the fire with a paper plate or frisbee.

To add a little extra flavor to whatever you are cooking, try burning something aromatic on the coals. Hickory chips or fruitwood add to the aroma and flavor. You can buy these chips commercially. To use, just follow the directions on the package. If you feel particularly innovative, experiment with sprinkling various herbs on the coals.

Controlling the Heat

The briquets will be a glowing white when they are ready for cooking. In the evening they will appear to be red. A briquet that is not quite hot enough will have a black area in its center. Once they are glowing, spread out the briquets so that you can begin cooking on them. The real key to barbecuing is learning how to control the heat. You can adjust the temperature by rearranging the briquets or by changing the distance of the rack from the glowing briquets.

A simple way to judge the relative temperature of a fire is to place your hand above the charcoal briquets at about the heigth at which your food will cook. If you can count three seconds (saying slowly, "One thousand, two thousand, three thousand . . .") before having to take away your hand, you have a *very hot* fire—about 400 to 500 degrees F. If you can count to six thousand, you have a *hot* fire—300 to 400 degrees F.

To make a *very* hot fire, place the briquets side by side and touching. When you're placing a cooking container over the charcoal briquets, you will need only a hot fire. Arrange the briquets in a checkerboard pattern, leaving as much space between each charcoal briquet as the width of the briquet. This arrangement will make the heat just right for cooking with a pan. Be sure to check your food while it is cooking to see that the heat is not too intense.

As the charcoal briquets burn down, they will form a white ash on the outside, which also causes them to cool. If you need more heat from them, tap the briquets lightly with a pair of tongs. Once they are half burned down, move them closer together to increase the heat.

Adding Briquets

When adding briquets to a well-established bed of briquets, place them at the edges. Adding them to the center immediately reduces the heat. If you are cooking a large piece of meat such as a turkey or a roast, you will need additional fuel, and having a small brazier or hibachi filled with hot coals ready to add to the large barbecue is a great help.

Controlling Flare-Ups

One of the main problems people have while cooking meats over charcoal briquets is controlling flare-ups. Flare-ups are caused by grease dripping onto the charcoal briquets and then catching fire. The flames blacken the food you are cooking, giving it an unpleasant taste. A good way to help avoid flare-ups is to trim as much fat from meat as possible and to buy extra-lean hamburger. You may want to use a spray bottle to control flare-ups by squirting a fine spray over the area that is flaring up. If you have children around, borrow a squirt gun; it is also very effective. Or tie the end of a cloth to the end of a stick or broom handle, dip the rag in water, and touch it to the areas that flare up. If you have a grill with a lid, cover the grill and close the vents to control flare-ups. Remember, however, that the goal is not to cool the charcoal, but rather only to try to control the flames.

Another tip: If you are serving a green salad, drop some of the outer leaves of the lettuce onto the areas that flare up. Lettuce is about 95 percent moisture and will quickly suffocate a flare-up caused by dripping meat. Table salt is also effective in controlling flare-ups.

Reusing Charcoal Briquets

It is wasteful to let charcoal briquets burn until completely out. Learn to save them when you are finished cooking. Briquets can be used three to four times if they are doused as soon as you are through cooking with them.

There are two ways to stop briquets from burning. One is to douse them with water or to place them in water with a pair of tongs. The other method involves cutting off oxygen by placing the charcoal briquets in a can and covering them with a metal lid. On dome grills, put on the lid and close all vents to smother the briquets. If water is used to douse burning briquets, dry them out completely before you reuse them. Briquets that have already been used should not be placed back into a charcoal marinating can, because they will break into small pieces and collect on the bottom. Instead, place them on cement or blacktop and let them dry out. Then add them to the top of the pyramid when you light the charcoal briquets on your next cookout.

Using Gas Barbecues

One alternative to briquets is a commercial gas grill. Depending on the type of gas barbecue you have, there are several ways to regulate heat. Some models have control knobs with high, medium, and low settings (the high setting is about 500 degrees F., medium 400 degrees F., and low 300 degrees F.). You can check the exact temperature of your gas grill by purchasing an oven thermometer at the grocery store. Place the thermometer in the center of the rack and close the door ten minutes, then read.

Grill lids can be closed to create an oven effect. The heat can be lowered inside the "oven" by raising the lid. Some grills have lids with built-in notches for this purpose. Otherwise, use rocks or bricks to prop open the grill lid.

Control flare-ups on gas grills in the same way you would when using a conventional barbecue.

3. Stick Cooking

Almost everyone has had the opportunity to roast a hot dog over coals or toast marshmallows over glowing embers. In fact, when you mention outdoor cooking, that is all many people have ever tried. But the items that can be cooked on a stick or spit, sometimes called a rotisserie, are almost limitless. With some imagination and creativity, you can come up with all sorts of combinations that are lip-smacking delicious.

There are two ways of using a stick for cooking. One is to place food on the end of the stick, and then hold the stick over the coals and rotate it as the food cooks, or place kebabs on the grill. This method is used for items that require a short cooking time. The second method, spit cooking, is used for larger items that require longer cooking, such as chicken, Cornish hens, turkeys, or even suckling pig. The item is placed on a large stick or metal rod that holds it above the coals while it is rotated. A rotisserie unit can be purchased commercially or improvised. Motorized units are available if you don't want to turn the spit by hand.

Principles of Stick Cooking

Stick cooking is similar to cooking on the broiler of a kitchen range. The larger the item—and the deeper the heat must penetrate—the farther away from the coals the stick is held. Items that are placed very close to the heat cook quickly on the outside but not on the inside. Placed

Food on metal and wooden skewers held over coals to cook.

close to or in the flames, most foods will burn easily while remaining raw inside. For instance, small items, such as marshmallows, can be placed very close to the coals and will cook quickly, while bread dough wrapped around a stick should not be held too close to the coals, or it will blacken on the outside while remaining doughy inside.

Skewers and Sticks

Several different types of commercial skewers and sticks are available for cooking. Some can be constructed at home from materials around the house. If you buy small bamboo skewers, you should soak them in water before you use them, to prevent them from burning. If you would rather make a skewer yourself, simply straighten out a coat hanger, put three or four empty spools on the bottom for a handle, pull the wire through the centers of the spools and wind it up around to secure them. Before using your skewer, place it in coals or fire to let any paint burn off. After it has cooled, rub it with fine steel wool. Whenever you use a metal skewer, you can clean it easily by putting it back in the coals to burn off the drippings. When cool, wipe off, and it will be ready to use again. You can also fashion a stick from a dowel by sharpening one end with a pocket knife or pencil sharpener. When you use wood or bamboo skewers or sticks, soak them in water for several hours before using them so they will not burn.

Since this stick or spit method of cooking uses dry heat which does not tenderize meat as do moist cooking methods, plan to use tender cuts of meat, ground beef balls, or less tender cuts of meat that can be cut into small boneless pieces and marinated.

Meat cuts to use include:

Beef Cuts

Filet mignon or tenderloin steak (cubed)
Top sirloin steak (cubed)
Porterhouse steak (cubed)
T-bone steak
New York-cut steak

Spencer or rib eye steak
Rib steak
Blade—chuck steak
Ground-beef balls
Liver

Pork Cuts

Pork chops, cubed
   Loin chop
   Rib chop
   Sirloin chop
   Blade chop

Pork tenderloin, cubed
Ham, cubed
Link or rolled sausages
Bacon—use to wrap around
   other pieces

Fish

Fillet, cubed
Whole fish, boned and cubed
Smoked fish

Oysters, plain or smoked
Shrimp—three inches or
   bigger

Other Meats

Chicken or turkey breasts
   (regular or smoked)
Luncheon meats, cubed, or
   wrap around other pieces

Wieners—turkey, beef,
   or pork
Pressed canned meat,
   cubed

Recipes

Hot Dogs on a Stick

For hot-dog lovers, there is probably no more delicious way to prepare them than over coals. Simply pierce the hot dog through with a wooden stick and rotate it over the coals to cook. Even very small children enjoy cooking their own hot dogs on sticks.

If you want to vary the traditional hot dog, try slitting the frankfurter down the center, being careful not to cut it in half. Fold thin slices of cheese and place them inside the split hot dog. Then wrap a thin slice of bacon around the hot dog, and secure with a toothpick. Skewer the wrapped hot dog onto a stick and toast over the coals. When it is juicy and hot, serve it on a hot dog bun with your favorite garnishes.

Another favorite variation combines hot dogs and biscuits in a delicious treat. Naturally, it is called:

Dog Biscuits

10 frankfurters   1 package of refrigerated
                                   biscuits

Secure franks on skewer. Using one biscuit per frank, roll each biscuit between your palms into a flat, 4-by-4-inch piece. Completely enclose frank in biscuit dough. Pinch tightly at each end to secure. Toast over coals, turning slowly to bake completely through until evenly browned (5 to 10 minutes).

Yield: 10 hot dogs

Variations: Cut frankfurter nearly through, fold open, and stuff middle with cheddar cheese, bleu cheese, Swiss cheese, pickles, sauerkraut, or even a little bit of chili. Mix Parmesan cheese into biscuit dough. Wrap frank in dough.

Kebabs

Intriguing and taste-tempting kebabs can be served as a main dish, salad, or even dessert. The nice thing about this food is that many different bite-sized foods can be arranged on serving plates and everyone can take turns assembling his own favorite combinations.

Basic Principles for Perfect Kebabs

If you want your kebabs to be tasty and attractive, be sure to choose foods that require about the same cooking

Double skewer.

time. Combining foods that cook at different rates may result in part of the kebab burning and falling into the fire while the rest is still half-cooked. If you want to use foods that take little cooking, such as cherry tomatoes or bananas, with other, longer-cooking foods, add the faster-cooking foods at the end of the cooking time, just a few minutes before you are ready to serve the kebabs. Also, avoid using small pieces of food that might pop or split when they are placed on the skewer.

One trick for creating easy-to-handle kebabs is to thread the items directly through their centers so they can't flop to their heavy side. If you have many irregularly shaped items that will flop around on the stick, you may need to use a double skewer to hold them. A handy way to construct a double skewer is to push two commerical skewers or two lengths of heavy wire or coat hanger (with paint burned off) into a large cork about ¼-inch apart. You can then thread the parallel skewers through the food.

Another hint for perfect kebabs is to leave a small space between the foods so they will cook more evenly and can be more thoroughly coated with sauce. If you are using foods that have fat on them, one way to prevent flare-ups is to place the charcoal briquets in rows approximately two inches apart and then cook the kebabs above the space between the rows so the drippings run into the empty area. The charcoal briquets will roast them as well as if the kebabs were suspended directly above the coals.

Meat Kebabs

For meat kebabs, be sure to use meat that is tender. Since stick cooking is a dry method of cooking and meat needs moisture to tenderize, the meat will not become tender as it cooks. Marinate less-tender cuts of meat for several hours at room temperature or a day ahead in the refrigerator, before cooking to help make them less chewy and more flavorful.

For a tasty kebab "sandwich," try nestling lettuce in pocket bread (pita), then filling the lettuce-lined pocket with kebab-cooked meat combinations. Add a squeeze of lemon, and you will have a refreshing sandwich.

Kebab sandwich.

Captivating Kebabs

Not only are these skewered meat, vegetable, and fruit combinations quick and easy to fix, but they will tickle the pickiest palate. You can put them on a grill to cook, turning them for even cooking, suspend them over the coals on bricks or stones, or hold them over the fire yourself.

Meatball Wrap-Up

A gourmet's delight!

1 pound ground beef
1 egg
½ cup dry bread crumbs
2 tablespoons Parmesan
  cheese
Salt

Pinch of oregano
½ pound sliced bacon
1 2-ounce can button mushrooms or ¼ pound fresh
  mushrooms
Cherry tomatoes (optional)

Mix beef, egg, bread crumbs, oregano, and cheese together and form into balls. Pre-cook meatballs in large frying pan until just cooked through.

Alternate cooked meatballs wrapped in bacon slices with mushrooms on skewer. Add cherry tomatoes for color. Cook over coals until bacon is cooked.

Yield: 8–10 kebabs

Beef and Cheese

Yummy!

1½ pounds tender beef, cut in
  small cubes
1 pound sliced bacon, cut in
  half

24–30 cubes Swiss cheese, cut
  bite size

Wrap cubes of cheese with half slices of bacon. Thread on skewer, alternating with cubes of beef. Cook four to five inches from coals for 30 minutes or until meat is done.

Yield: 8–10 kebabs

Oyster Roll-Up

Absolutely delicious!

1 3½-ounce can smoked oysters
½ pound sliced bacon, cut in half

1 pound round steak, cut in 1-inch cubes
1 3½-ounce can ripe olives

Wrap oysters in half slices of bacon. Alternate with steak cubes and ripe olives. Cook over hot coals approximately 30 minutes.

Yield: 8–10 kebabs

Shrimp on a Stick

A meal in itself.

1 4½-ounce can shrimp or 12 large fresh raw shrimp
¼ cup soy sauce
½ pound sliced bacon, cut in half

1 pound tender beef, cut in cubes
2 oranges, divided into wedges

Marinate shrimp in soy sauce for about 10 minutes, then wrap in halved-bacon slices. Thread on skewers, alternating with beef cubes and orange wedges. Cook over coals 20 to 25 minutes or until meat is cooked through.

Yield: 8–10 servings

Seafood Special

Super for sailors.

1 3½–4-ounce can smoked
   oysters
½ pound bacon

1 whole fish, filleted, boned,
   cut in cubes
1 lemon, cut in thin slices

Lemon Butter

Mix together:

¼ cup butter, melted
2 tablespoons lemon juice

2 teaspoons chopped fresh
   parsley

Wrap oysters in bacon. Alternate on skewer with cubes of fish and lemon slices. Brush kebab heavily with lemon butter. Cook four inches from coals for 15 to 20 minutes, basting often.

Yield: 6–8 kebabs

Shrimp on a stick.

Turkey Kebabs

Colorful and taste-tempting!

2 cups cooked turkey, cut in
    1-inch cubes
Curry powder

½ pound sliced bacon, cut in
    half
1 10-ounce can ripe olives
16–18 cherry tomatoes

Sprinkle turkey cubes with curry powder. Toss lightly to coat. Wrap each in one-half-slice bacon. Alternate on skewer with olives and tomatoes. Cook over hot coals about 5 to 10 minutes or until meat is thoroughly heated.

Yield: 8–10 kebabs

Ham-and-Chicken Kebab

A great meal or do-it-yourself kebab.

2 chicken breasts, skinned,
    boned, and cut in 1½-inch
    cubes
½ pound cooked ham, cut in
    1½-inch cubes

1 16-ounce can chunk pine-
    apple (use fresh fruit in
    season)
1 green pepper, cut in squares
Soy sauce
Pineapple juice
Cherry tomatoes (optional)

Alternate chicken and ham with pineapple chunks and green pepper squares on skewer. Brush with a mixture of soy sauce and pineapple juice. Cook over coals 25 to 30 minutes, or until meat is done, basting several times while cooking. Add cherry tomatoes.

Yield: 8–10 servings

Ham and chicken kebab.

Ham Kebabs Supreme

Fun and tasty!

12 thin slices of ham
Mustard
1 6-ounce can ripe olives

10–12 cocktail onions
3–4 cherry tomatoes (optional)

Spread each ham slice with mustard. Fold into bite-sized piece, mustard side in, and place on skewer, alternating with olives and onions. Cook over coals until ham is warmed through. Garnish with cherry tomatoes.

Yield: 6–8 kebabs

Hawaiian Ham and Cheese

Tangy and tantalizing!

8–10 thin slices of ham, cut in 1-inch strips
¼ pound Swiss cheese, cut in cubes

1 10–13 ounce can pineapple chunks or small fresh pineapple, cut in bite-size chunks
Green olives (optional)

Wrap ham strips around cheese cubes and thread on skewer, alternating with pineapple chunks. Add green olives. Cook three to four inches above hot coals for approximately 5 minutes. When cheese is melted and starts dripping, kebab is done.

Yield: 6 kebabs

Italian Pork Kebabs

This is a super meal. Add any other vegetable for great results.

1½ pounds pork, cut in 1-inch cubes
1 8-ounce bottle Italian salad dressing

1 4-ounce can mushroom buttons
6 tomatoes, cut in wedges
1 medium zucchini, cut in 1-inch pieces

Marinate pork in Italian dressing at least two hours at room temperature or overnight, if possible in refrigerator. Thread on skewer, alternating with vegetables. Grill four inches from heat for 20 to 30 minutes, until pork is cooked through.

Yield: 6 kebabs

Pork and Pineapple

A meal in itself!

1 pound pork tenderloin in bite-size cubes

1 10–13 ounce can pineapple chunks (use fresh fruit in season)

2 apples, peeled and cut in bite-size pieces

1 5-ounce bottle of tiny cocktail onions

¼ cup butter, melted

Cherry tomatoes (optional)

Thread meat, fruits, and vegetables in desired order on skewer. Brush with butter. Cook over hot coals 20 to 25 minutes, until pork is cooked through. Garnish with cherry tomatoes.

Yield: 8–10 kebabs

Tropical Bacon Kebab

Brings the lush tropics home.

6 slices bacon

1 13-ounce can pineapple chunks (use fresh fruit in season)

4 bananas, cut in chunks

6 maraschino cherries (optional)

Weave one strip bacon around 3 cubes of pineapple, 2 banana chunks, add a cherry and slide onto skewer. Cook over hot coals about 2 minutes, or until bacon is done, turning as needed.

Yield: 6 kebabs

Pepperoni and Olive Kebab

Beautiful and good!

1 3-ounce package large-sliced   1 green pepper cut in bite-size
   pepperoni   chunks
1 6-ounce can ripe olives

Wrap pepperoni halfway around ripe olive. Thread together on skewer. Continue, alternating placement of pepperoni with green pepper chunks. Cook over hot coals 4 to 6 minutes. Garnish with cherry tomatoes.

Yield: 6–8 kebabs

Dog-Gone-Its

Favorite frankfurters made better yet.

10 frankfurters, cut in   16 cherry tomatoes
   bite-size chunks   16 cocktail onions

Alternate meat and vegetables on skewer. Cook four inches from coals for 5 to 7 minutes.

Yield: 8 kebabs

Frankfurter Kebab

Great and easy luncheon kebab that is fun for children.

6 frankfurters, cut in   16 bologna or salami, slices
   bite-size chunks   cut in strips and rolled up
                             16 bite-size chunks of dill
                             pickle

Alternate ingredients on skewer. Cook four inches from coals for 4 to 6 minutes until franks are cooked.

Yield: 8 kebabs

Polish Kebab

Colorful and scrumptious.

2 Polish sausages, cut in
  ½-inch slices

12–14 cherry tomatoes
1 6-ounce can green olives

Alternate meat and vegetables on skewer. Cook four inches from hot coals 15 to 20 minutes, until sausage is cooked.

Yield: 6–8 kebabs

German Gourmet

Watch them line up for more!

4 knockwurst sausages, cut in
  1-inch slices
12 parboiled potatoes, cut in
  1-inch slices

12 small cocktail onions
12 green olives (optional)
¼ cup melted butter

Thread ingredients on skewers. Brush with melted butter. Cook four inches from coals for 15 to 20 minutes.

Yield: 4–6 kebabs

Luncheon Surprise

A different combination that will definitely please.

1 20-ounce can pineapple
  chunks (use fresh fruit in
  season)
6 slices luncheon-meat, cut in
  1½-inch strips

3 bananas, peeled and cut in
  chunks
¼ cup butter, melted

Wrap pineapple in luncheon-meat strips. Alternate with banana chunks. Brush with melted butter. Cook over coals until meat is warmed through.

Stuffed mushrooms.

You may also add cheese of any kind. When using cheese, use two bamboo skewers side by side one-fourth inch apart. Or wrap cheese with bacon and pierce each end of stuffed bacon roll with one skewer so the cheese won't ooze out while the bacon is cooking.

Yield: 6 kebabs

Stuffed Mushrooms

Better than you think mushrooms can be!

18–20 medium-sized mushrooms
1 2½-ounce can deviled ham

1 5-ounce jar cocktail onions
9–10 cherry tomatoes
¼ cup melted butter

Remove stems from mushrooms. Fill caps with deviled ham. Place two caps together facing each other and thread on skewer. Alternate double mushroom caps with onions and tomatoes. Brush with melted butter. Cook four inches from coals for 15 to 20 minutes, until mushrooms are tender.

Yield: 8–10 kebabs

Garden Delight

Here's something delightful straight from the garden.

12 small parboiled potatoes
12 cherry tomatoes

1 large green pepper, cut into bite-size squares
12 small cocktail onions

Alternate vegetables on skewer. Cook only until warmed through if you like your pepper a little crunchy, or a little longer, 4 to 5 minutes, for more tender vegetables. Cook about four inches from the coals.

Yield: 4–6 servings

Dessert on a Stick

These sweet treats blend fruit and dessert into delicious surprises.

Cherry-Coconut Cake

Super dessert!

1 small pound cake, cut in cubes
1 8–8½-ounce jar apricot, strawberry, or cherry jam or preserves
1 cup shredded coconut
1 8-ounce jar maraschino cherries

Spread jam on all sides of cubes of pound cake. Roll in coconut. Thread cake on skewer alternating with maraschino cherries. Roast over coals until coconut is browned.

Yield: 6–8 servings

Heavenly Toast

The best! Easy and delicious.

1 loaf day-old bread, unsliced
1 13-ounce can sweetened condensed milk
1½ cups grated coconut

Cut bread into 2-inch cubes. Place bread securely on skewers. Dip bread in sweetened condensed milk, then into coconut, coating evenly. Toast until coconut is brown and bread is warmed through. Watch carefully so coconut doesn't burn.

Yield: 8–10 servings

Cherry-coconut cake.

Bread on a Stick

A crusty outside yields a soft surprise inside.

2 cups Bisquick mix   1 tablespoon vegetable oil
½ cup water

Mix Bisquick and water to form soft dough. Pinch off a small portion of dough and mold it into a long patty. Wrap it around the end of a 1-inch-thick dowel stick that has been oiled. Be sure dough covers end of stick. Roast over coals slowly. When done, slip off stick and fill hole with: butter and jelly, pie filling, diced cheese, or peanut butter. This recipe will become a family favorite for breakfast, lunch, or dessert.

Yield: 10–12 servings

Apple on a Stick

So tasty you will think it's Mom's baked apple.

1 apple per person   2 tablespoons cinnamon
2 cups sugar

Mix sugar and cinnamon together and place in shallow bowl. Place apple on end of stick and rotate over glowing coals until it becomes shiny and skin begins to pop. Remove from fire, cool slightly and peel apple. Roll in sugar and cinnamon, and place back over coals until the sugar begins to melt and drip off apple. Remove and cut slice off and then repeat process until apple is gone.

Variation: Peel and slice apple into chunks. Place on skewer, brush with butter and roll into sugar and cinnamon. Toast over glowing coals.

Banana-Nut Kebabs

Taste meets texture and creates delight.

4 bananas, peeled and cut in   ½ cup mixed chopped nuts
    quarters   (peanuts, walnuts, and
¼ cup butter, melted   pecans)
                                     4–8 maraschino cherries
                                        (optional)

Dip bananas in butter and thread on skewers. Add cherries. Roast over coals until warmed through, then roll in chopped nuts and enjoy.

Yield: 4 servings

Cherry-Peach Kebabs

Peaches like you've never tasted before.

1 16-ounce can peach halves
  (use fresh fruit in season)
Maraschino cherries

1 5¼-ounce can pineapple
  chunks (use fresh fruit in
  season)
¼ cup butter, melted

Quarter peach halves. Alternate fruit, beginning and ending skewer with pineapple chunks. Cook over coals, brushing often with butter. Note: If double skewers are used, they will help hold the fruit on more securely.

Yield: 4–6 servings

Donut Holes and Fruit

Delicious and filling.

1 dozen donut holes
1 package marshmallows
1 20-ounce can pineapple
  chunks (use fresh fruit in
  season)

Maraschino cherries
1 16-ounce can peaches (use
  fresh fruit in season) sliced
  and cut in 1½ inch cubes

Alternate ingredients on skewer and cook over hot coals until marshmallows are toasted. Eat while hot.

Yield: 3–4 kebabs

Ginger Pineapple

Try the ginger butter with other fruits, too.

½ cup melted butter
2 tablespoons sugar
½ teaspoon ginger

1 20-ounce can pineapple
  chunks (use fresh fruit in
  season)
½ cup coconut flakes

Mix melted butter, sugar, and ginger together to make ginger butter. Dip pineapple in ginger butter and roll in coconut. Place on skewer and toast over coals until coconut is brown. Other fresh fruit can be added along with pineapple, if desired.

Yield: 4–6 servings

Shaggy Dogs

A new way to enjoy stick cooking.

1 package large
  marshmallows

1 cup chocolate or caramel
  syrup
1 cup coconut

Roast each marshmallow until golden brown. Dip into syrup, roll in coconut and eat.

Spit Cooking

Whether you are cooking a chicken, a Cornish game hen, or even a small roast or ham, you will want to try cooking on a spit. Rotisserie cooking provides an ideal method for involving guests in the cooking. If you choose the carefree route—a mechanical rotisserie that turns by itself—all you have to do is baste.

Improvised Spits

Dowels make convenient spits; however, the wood is usually so slick that it is best to drill holes along the center of the dowel so the food can be wired onto the dowel. Wiring the food to the spit will keep it from flopping to the heavy side and not cooking.

A metal pipe can also be used as a spit. Again, drill holes

Spit supported with bricks.

Spit supported on metal pipe with rungs.

through the middle for fastening food. Galvanized metal pipes (metal with a coating on it) should not be used for cooking because they are coated with a substance that can be harmful when heated.

Supports for Spits

Supports for spits can be made in a variety of ways. One of the easiest is to use a few bricks, or cement blocks, preferably the type that have holes in the center. Place the bricks on the opposite sides of the coals where the spit is to be supported and then suspend the spit across the middle. Place two sticks vertically through two holes in each brick to keep the spit from rolling off. Again, you can control the temperature easily by removing or adding bricks. (To raise the heat, remove a brick. To lower the heat, place another brick underneath, raising the food higher above the coals.)

Another method of suspending the spit is to place flat rocks on top of each other to form supports above the coals. Or use two pieces of board, placing nails along the edge of the boards and bending the nails up so that a dowel spit can be suspended on the rungs formed by the nails. Place nails every two or three inches so the stick can be raised or lowered as the temperature needs to be adjusted. A similar spit can be made from two metal pipes by welding small rungs or ledges onto it so that the spit can be suspended from the metal rungs. You should plan to weld at least two or three rungs or ledges to each pipe so the stick holding the food can be raised or lowered as the cooking heat needs to be adjusted.

Use your ingenuity to find other items around the house to create spits for cooking in your backyard.

Meats to Cook on Your Spit

Since this method of cooking uses dry heat, you will want to use large, tender cuts of meat such as:

Beef Cuts

Rib roast
Sirloin tip roast
Top round roast (same as top
   round steak, but cut thicker).
   Extremely good if you like beef rare.

Pork

Ham or pork roast (the pork requires
   special care to cook well all
   the way through)

Other Meats

Whole turkey
Whole chicken
Cornish game hen
Game birds

Ready, Set, Cook

Prepare the food you want to cook on the spit, along with
the marinade or sauce you are going to use for basting.
Secure food on the spit, centering it so that it will turn
evenly. It is a good idea to wire food to the spit if you don't
have the kind of commercial rotisserie that secures the
food with metal prongs. Be sure to secure wings and legs
of poultry tightly to the meat so that they do not burn. A
quick check for an evenly balanced skewer is to suspend the
loaded skewer in the crook of your hand between thumb
and forefinger. If the skewer rolls backward easily, it is
evenly balanced.

Suspend food on the spit over cooking coals and begin
turning. The average piece of meat should cook about eight
to ten inches from the coals. Larger pieces will need to be
farther away, and smaller pieces closer. Check the meat
often so that if it is cooking too quickly or too slowly, you
can raise or lower the spit. Make sure the meat continues
to rotate slowly. Food that needs to cook a long time should
be rotated on a 3-to-5-minute basis.

You may want to baste the meat with marinade or barbecue sauce as it cooks. If you use a basting sauce that contains tomato or brown sugar, do not begin basting until the meat is almost cooked—the last 15 minutes—because brown sugar and tomato cause the surface of the meat to burn.

4. Foil Cooking

Foil is a great invention for the outdoor cook, since it allows you to create individual pans to fit your food. Handy and practical as well, foil eliminates the need to clean dishes.

Foil wrap comes in two different widths, 12 inches and 18 inches. There are three different weights. The thinnest foil weight is usually not practical for cooking items over coals unless double wrapped because it is too easy to puncture. Heavy-duty foil makes excellent foil packages for outdoor cooking. For especially heavy jobs—or when you want to improvise your own foil pans—use extra-heavy-duty foil.

One of the handier uses of foil in outdoor cooking is to wrap the food so it can be set directly on coals. Cut a piece of foil large enough to allow four to six inches of overlap on each side of your food item. Place the food in the center of the foil, then bring the two opposite sides together at the top of the food and roll down in small folds. Flatten the two remaining sides of foil and roll in small folds toward the food. This type of wrapping is called the "drugstore wrap." With most cooking projects, heavy-duty foil using the drugstore wrap is sufficient to seal in juices and provide trouble-free cooking.

Foil is also useful when you wish to keep food from browning too much. For example, if you are cooking a chicken over a spit, or roasting a turkey on a vertical spit, and the bird is already golden brown, wrap it in foil so that you can continue to roast it until it has finished cooking. The foil will keep the food from burning.

Drugstore wrap (1).

Drugstore wrap (2).

Foil also comes in preshaped pans sold commercially. These disposable pans are excellent for cooking such foods as fruit upside-down cake, and for constructing an "oven" by clamping two foil pie tins together with a metal clamp on each side. Suspend the clamped tins above a few coals, then place a few more coals on top. Do not use a solid bed of briquets below the pans because it will generate too much heat. Use the foil-pan "oven" for cooking or warming food.

One caution about foil: Since it is very thin, the heat of charcoal briquets can easily burn food cooked in foil unless you are careful. For example, when cooking a hamburger inside foil, you can place food with a high amount of moisture, such as onions, lettuce, potatoes, or carrots, on both

87

Foil-packaged foods cooking on racks above coals.

sides of the hamburger. Since these foods contain about 90 percent moisture, the vegetables give off steam which helps to prevent the surface of the meat from scorching.

A convenient way of insulating the package itself is to wrap the foil package in newspaper. Place the food to be cooked on the foil and use the drugstore wrap method for securing it. Then cut strips of newspaper the size of the package and wrap around the outside of the foil package until you have about ⅛-inch-thick layer of newspapers. Vary the thickness of the layer according to the intensity of the coals and what you are cooking. Wrap the package again in foil, then place above the coals. The newspapers provide an insulating layer between the food and the coals. Wet newspaper can also be wrapped around the first foil wrap and then placed on the coals. This method is good for foods that have a short cooking time, such as fish. The paper will be almost dry enough to flame when the food inside the foil is done. Remove before paper catches fire.

If you don't want to insulate your foil package, you can prevent burning by suspending a rack on bricks two inches above the coals. Cook your foil-wrapped food on the rack, turning at least once.

Foil is particularly well suited to cooking vegetables. Butter and wrap potatoes in foil, for instance, and place them in the coals before you put your steaks on to cook. You can also wrap squash, onions, peas, carrots, and many other vegetables in foil and cook them with your meat or separately.

As you begin to use foil, you will find more and more ways to use it in your backyard cooking. Food cooked in foil can be served in it, too, by brushing the ashes off the foil and turning the package seam down. With a knife, cut an X from corner to corner in the foil package, pull back the foil, and eat your delicious meal right out of the foil.

Since foil cooking uses moist heat, less-tender cuts of meat may be used as well as tender cuts. For example, try these beef cuts: round steak, flank steak, chuck steak, and pot roast. For fish try whole fish or smoked fish. Turkey, chicken, hot dogs, and any meats normally steamed or cooked in liquids in the oven or a tightly covered pan on the top of the stove will make excellent choices for foil cooking.

Foil-Cooked Recipes

These delicious main dishes combine tempting goodness with outdoor heartiness. And, since they cook in their own foil pans, they help eliminate those after-dinner dish-washing blues.

Chip 'n Dip Chicken

A backyard or patio dish that's easy on the beginner cook.

6 meaty chicken breasts or legs
Dash salt
Dash pepper

1 8-ounce carton of onion chip dip
1½ cups crushed potato chips

Season pieces of chicken with salt and pepper. Spread each piece generously with chip dip and roll in crushed potato chips. Place two servings on a 12-by-18-inch piece of foil and wrap, using the drugstore wrap. Place on a wire rack two to three inches above the glowing coals or charcoal, or wrap in insulated foil package, and cook directly on coals for 20 minutes on each side.

Yield: 6 servings

Chicken Cordon Bleu Supreme

Very elegant!

6 whole chicken breasts	Dash pepper
1 5-ounce package sliced ham	¼ cup butter or margarine
4 ounces Swiss cheese	½ cup bread crumbs
½ teaspoon leaf thyme	4 strips bacon
¼ teaspoon salt	

Skin and bone each chicken breast, then flatten to ⅛-inch thickness by pounding with flat side of meat mallet or a rolling pin. Place one slice of ham over each breast. Cut cheese into thin strips and cover ham. Sprinkle with thyme, salt, and pepper. Roll chicken and ham around cheese, tucking in the ends and pressing to seal well. Roll in butter, then in breadcrumbs to cover. Wrap a slice of bacon around the chicken and put toothpicks through both sides to secure. (Clip the ends of the picks so they won't puncture foil.) Wrap in foil, using the drugstore wrap. Place on wire grill two to three inches above glowing coals or charcoals, or insulate the foil package and place directly over the coals for 15 to 20 minutes on each side.

Yield: 4 servings

Barbecue Drumsticks

A unique variation of everyone's favorite meatloaf.

1 pound ground beef	¼ cup barbecue sauce
1 teaspoon salt	1 egg
¼ teaspoon pepper	breadcrumbs
1 small onion, chopped	6 slices bacon

Mix together the ground beef, salt, pepper, onion, barbecue sauce, and egg. Divide into six equal portions. Form portions into a four-inch rectangular shape around end of skewer, then roll in breadcrumbs and place ½ slice of bacon on each side of the drumstick. Place on a 10-by-18-inch piece of foil and wrap using the drugstore wrap, twisting the end around the stick. Hold above coals or place on a wire grill two to three inches above the glowing coals or charcoal, or insulate the foil package and cook on glowing coals for 20 minutes on each side. Serve.

Yield: 6 servings

Onion Meatloaf

Meatloaf that's sure to please the heartiest appetites!

1 pound ground beef	⅛ teaspoon pepper
1 egg	6 large onions
½ teaspoon salt	

Mix ground beef, egg, salt and pepper. Cut six onions in half horizontally and remove middle sections. Divide meatloaf into six portions and fill onion cups. Put the two onion halves back together. Place on piece of foil. Wrap, using the drugstore wrap, and cook directly on coals

15 minutes on each side. (The onions contain enough moisture to keep the meat from overcooking.)

Yield: 6 servings

Trout in Foil

There's no better way to eat 'em after you've caught 'em.

1 trout	Juice of ½ lemon
1 tablespoon butter	Salt and pepper to taste

Remove fins and head of the fish. Rub with butter, salt, and pepper. Place on a sheet of 12-by-18-inch heavy-duty foil. Wrap, using drugstore wrap. Place on wire grill two to three inches above glowing coals or charcoal. Or insulate the foil package and place directly on the coals. Cook about 20 minutes on each side. Serve with lemon juice.

Yield: 1 serving

Deboning a Trout: After trout has been cooked in foil, take a knife and cut along the backbone of the fish. Carefully lift both sides of the fish away from the bone. Firmly hold the tail and lift it up carefully, letting the meat drop away from the bone. If the trout is well cooked, the fish will come clean of the bones. This method of deboning will work with any fresh-water fish.

Kraut-Dog Dinner

A zesty taste-bud treat that's quick and easy.

1 16-ounce can sauerkraut	½ pound Swiss cheese
8 hot dogs	

Cut four pieces of heavy-duty foil, each 12 by 18 inches. Divide the sauerkraut into four equal portions on foil. Split hot dogs down the center and place wedges of Swiss cheese in splits. Use two hot dogs per foil. Place sauerkraut under and over the hot dogs. Seal foil, using the drugstore wrap. Cook on a wire rack two inches above the coals, or double-wrap and lay on coals. Cook 10 minutes on each side.

Yield: 4 two-dog servings

Golden Crown Potatoes

Potatoes were never better.

4 potatoes
½ cup sharp cheddar cheese, grated

1 large onion, chopped

Scrub potatoes and cut lengthwise. With melon baller, scoop six holes out of each half-potato. Fill four holes with sharp cheddar cheese and two with chopped onion. Place potato halves back together, wrap in foil using drugstore wrap. Place on wire grill two to three inches above glowing coals or charcoal, or insulate foil package. Place directly on coals and cook for 30 minutes per side.

Yield: 4 servings

French-Fried Potatoes in Foil

A melt-in-your-mouth potato dish, delicious and creamy.

4 medium baking potatoes, pared
3 tablespoons butter or margarine

1½ teaspoons salt
Dash pepper
1½ tablespoons chopped parsley
½ cup sour cream

Cut an 18-inch length of heavy-duty foil. Cut potatoes into French-fry slices and place in the center of the foil. Dot with butter, sprinkle with salt, pepper, and parsley. Wrap, using drugstore wrap, and place on wire grill two to three inches above glowing coals or charcoal, or insulate foil package and cook directly on the coals for 20 minutes on each side. Open foil, place in serving dish, cover with ½ cup of sour cream, sprinkle with additional parsley, and serve.

Yield: 4 servings

Mushroom-Onion Potatoes

Mouth-watering and easy!

6 medium potatoes
1 stick softened butter or
   margarine

1 envelope mushroom-onion
   soup mix

Scrub potatoes, leaving skins on. Slice potatoes in ¼-inch slices. Blend butter and soup mix and spread on each potato slice. Put potatoes back together and wrap in 12-by-12-inch heavy-duty aluminum foil, using the drugstore wrap. Place on grill two to three inches above the glowing coals or charcoal, or insulate foil package and cook directly on coals. Cook ½ hour on each side or until done.

Yield: 6 servings

Yam and Ham

A fabulous side dish or meal-in-one.

4 yams
1 cup chopped ham
1 cup pineapple chunks

⅓ cup brown sugar
¼ cup small marshmallows

Cut yams lengthwise and remove their centers with a fruit baller. Mix the ham, pineapple, and brown sugar, and place inside the hollowed-out yams. Put the two halves of the yams back together, wrap in foil, and place on wire grill two to three inches above the glowing coals or charcoal. Or wrap in insulated foil package, and place directly on the coals for 30 to 45 minutes per side. Open the foil, pull the yams apart, and place a few marshmallows in their centers. Put the yams back together, wrap in foil, and let sit for a few minutes until the marshmallows melt. Open and serve.

Yield: 4 servings

Mushrooms in Foil

A delicious accompaniment to any meat or poultry dish.

½ pound fresh mushrooms	½ teaspoon salt
2 tablespoons butter	½ teaspoon pepper

Slice mushrooms in half. Place on a piece of foil dotted with butter, and season with salt and pepper. Wrap mushrooms in foil, using the drugstore wrap, and place over the coals for about 5 minutes on each side.

Yield: 6–8 servings

Stuffed Mushrooms

A mushroom connoisseur's delight!

12 large mushrooms	3 tablespoons butter
2 tablespoons onion, finely chopped	¼ cup celery, minced
	½ cup grated cheese

Remove stems and centers from mushrooms with a measuring spoon. Mince stems. Sauté stem pieces, onion, and celery in butter until tender. Spoon mixture into the mushroom caps and sprinkle with cheese. Wrap two caps in foil and place on the back of the grill, stuffing side up, 12 to 15 minutes or until mushrooms are done. These can be prepared ahead of time, and refrigerated until ready to be cooked.

Yield: 6 servings.

Tomatoes Supreme

Delicious served as a side dish along with a tender steak!

½ pound fresh mushrooms	2 tablespoons butter
½ cup finely chopped onion	4 medium firm tomatoes

Sauté mushrooms and onions in butter until tender. Core the tomatoes and carefully scoop out the seeds. Fill the tomatoes with mushroom, onion, and butter mixture. Wrap in foil and place on the coals for 5 minutes, or until the tomatoes are barely warm. Do not overcook. This dish can be prepared ahead of time and left in the refrigerator overnight to be cooked at the same time you cook the main dish.

Yield: 4 servings

Fresh Corn on the Cob

Select tender, juicy ears of corn. Peel back the husks from the corn about one inch and remove the top silk. Pull husks back over the corn and soak in water for one hour. Wrap in foil, using drugstore wrap, and place on coals about 5 minutes per side. Unwrap, pull husk back, butter and season to taste.

Wheelbarrow salad bar and soda station.

Pitchfork skewers.

Ice bowl.

Wagon grill.

Double skewers.

Shovel frying pan.

Flowerpot grill.

Spit supported on metal pipes with rungs.

Ironing-board buffet.

Five-gallon newspaper stove.

Table setting held securely against breezes in windproof table cover.

Hibachi grill.

Food on metal and wood skewers.

Donut delight.

Cherry-coconut cakes.

Wheelbarrow set up for rotisserie, grill, and open-coals cooking.

Chinese Veg Pack

It tastes so good, you'll forget it's good for you!

1 stalk celery, thinly
  sliced on an angle
1 green pepper, cut in strips
6 large mushrooms, cut in half

1 medium onion, thinly sliced
1 tomato, sliced
3 teaspoons butter
Salt and pepper to taste

Place celery, green pepper, mushrooms, onions, and tomatoes on 15-by-18-inch piece of heavy-duty aluminum foil. Dot with butter, salt and pepper. Place on grill for 15 minutes per side or wrap in insulated foil package, and place on coals for 10 minutes per side.

Yield: 4 servings

Butternut Chop

A delicious way to an easy meal.

1 butternut squash
2 1-inch-thick pork chops,
  center cut

2 tablespoons butter
1 tablespoon brown sugar
Salt and pepper

Cut squash in half, scoop out seeds. Cut the hole big enough to fit the pork chop. Place butter and brown sugar in each half and salt and pepper. Place pork chop in the squash. Wrap, using the drugstore wrap. Place on wire grill two to three inches above glowing coals or charcoal, or wrap in insulated foil package, and cook directly on the coals for 45 minutes on each side. Cook the cut side up first so the butter cooks into the squash.

Yield: 2 servings

Butternut chops.

Foil-Wrapped Desserts

These delectable desserts are designed to satisfy your sweet tooth.

Hawaiian Banana Boats

No better way to end a meal!

6 bananas   ½ cup brown sugar
1 cup pineapple chunks   ½ cup shredded coconut

Cut a long wedge-shaped section on the banana. Pull back the peeling and eat the wedge. Fill the cavity with four or five chunks of pineapple, leaving a space between each. Fill half the spaces with brown sugar and the rest with coconut. Pull the banana skin back over the coconut-pineapple-filled wedge, wrap in foil, and place over the coals. Cook for 5 minutes, until the brown sugar is melted.

Yield: 6 servings

Variations: Fill the cavity with chocolate chips and miniature marshmallows or with butterscotch chips and miniature marshmallows. Or dream up your favorite combinations with bananas.

Dessert Apples

Remember how these tasted at the circus?

One apple is needed for each serving of this delicious dessert. Core the center of each apple, taking care not to cut all the way through the apple. Make the cavity large enough so that a filling can be placed into it. Fill with one of more of the following:

Brown sugar Nuts and raisins
Red hots Sugar and cinnamon mixture

Put the apple on a 12-by-12-inch piece of heavy-duty foil. Bring the foil to the top, twist it around, and place on a wire grill two to three inches above the glowing coals, or wrap in insulated foil package. Cook for 45 minutes, keeping the apple open-end up.

Orange-Cup Cakes

This great dessert will leave everyone begging for more.

Oranges, one for each serving   1 box cake mix (flavor of your
                                     choice)

Cut the top quarter off each orange. Carefully cut out orange, leaving peeling intact to form a cup. Mix cake batter according to package directions. Fill each orange cup two-thirds full of batter. Replace top of orange. Place each orange in the center of a 12-by-12-inch piece of heavy-duty foil. Bring foil up around the orange, then twist top of foil closed. Leave enough air in the foil for the cake to rise. Place on coals and cook 15 to 20 minutes, until cup cakes are done.

Yield: 1 cake mix package fills 15–20 oranges

5. Grills

Nothing sets the stage for an outdoor party better than steaks sizzling on a grill over hot, glowing coals. Three types of grills are available for preparing your steaks: wire, solid, or hinged basket.

The most common kind of grill is the wire grill that comes with a commercial barbecue. The best kind of grill is one that can be raised or lowered to regulate the heat and is large enough to hold servings for several people. If you

Cooking on a solid grill.

are improvising your own barbecue, an oven rack, a cookie-cooling rack, or even a heavy screen can be used for the grill. Although some racks—oven racks, for instance—have wires too far apart for grilling hamburgers, they are suitable for cooking steaks and other large items. A cookie-cooling rack, which has a narrow space between its wires, could be placed on top of the oven rack to allow for cooking both small and large items.

Using a solid grill or griddle is like cooking in a frying pan, only the griddle has a much greater surface. It is ideal for preparing early-morning pancakes or quick side dishes while you grill your steaks on a wire rack.

The hinged wire-basket grills are usually large enough to contain three or four pieces of chicken or a large steak. You can suspend the basket over the coals by placing a brick underneath each side.

Controlling the Heat

The key to cooking over a grill is learning how to regulate the grill to control heat. Heat is regulated over coals by changing the placement of your grilling rack. The farther the grill is from the coals, the slower the food will cook. Keep in mind that the average distance between the food and the coals should measure about four to six inches, and that food that is thick and needs to be well done should be moved farther away so that it cooks slowly and thoroughly. Food that is thin and can cook faster can be moved closer to the source of the heat. The cut of meat, its size and shape, and its temperature when placed on the grill all affect the amount of time required to cook it. Also, on a commercial bubble barbecue or a hibachi, air vents at the bottom regulate the amount of oxygen circulating around the coals. By closing the vents, you cut off oxygen and decrease the heat. Opening the vents increases the heat.

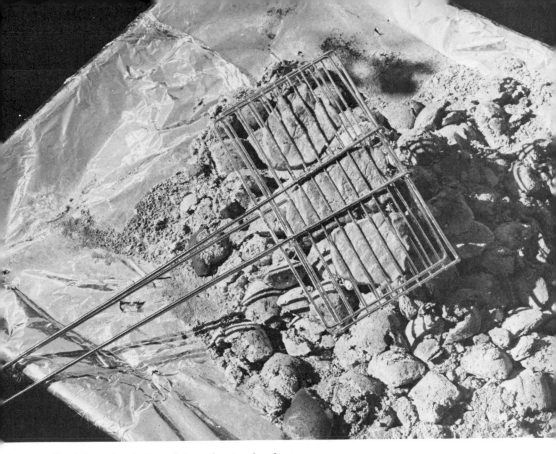
Cooking steak in a hinged wire basket.

Another heat regulator is proper use of coals. Coals are at their top temperature just after they become white. If they sit for half an hour to an hour, they will cool down a bit, because the ash that collects on the coals insulates them. If you need more heat, tap the white ash off the charcoals.

Grilling Meats

Grill cooking is a dry-heat method. Less-tender cuts of meat do not become tender as they do in moist cooking, so you will have to use tender cuts, ground-meat patties, or less-tender cuts that have been marinated or tenderized before grilling. Some good meats for grilling include:

Beef Cuts

Filet mignon or tenderloin steak
Top sirloin steak
Porterhouse steak
T-bone steak
New York or strip steak
Spencer or rib-eye steak
Rib steak
Blade chuck steak
Ground beef patties
Cuts to be marinated, such as
    flank steak, top round steak, and
    skirt steak rolls

Pork Cuts

Country-style spareribs
Regular spareribs
Back ribs
Pork chops, including
    loin chop, rib chop, sirloin chop, or
    blade chop
Pork tenderloin
Center-cut leg steak
Ham slices

Other

Whole fish or filets
Turkey parts
Chicken parts

Following these handy tips will help insure good grill cooking:

- Trim excess fat from the meat to eliminate flare-ups and use extra-lean hamburger.
- Thin steaks and chops will sometimes curl around the edges. Clipping the fat in about ½ inch deep along the edges eliminates this.
- Use tongs to turn a steak instead of a fork. Forks punch holes into the meat and cause the juices to run out.
- Brush food with oil before placing on a grill so that it doesn't stick to the grill, or brush grill with oil. The latter method provides fewer calories.
- Check doneness of a steak by making a thin cut into the center of the meat.
- It is usually best to season meat at the end of the cooking time so that the salt does not draw the juices out of the meat during the cooking process. The meat will be juicier when served.

Marinating or Tenderizing Meats: A Matter of Taste

If you are going to grill less tender cuts of meat, you will probably want to tenderize or marinate them before cooking. Marinating adds liquid to meats, which makes them more tender as well as making the meat more flavorful. You can also physically tenderize the meat or use a commercial tenderizer. To physically tenderize meat, tough cuts are ground up whole, and Swiss-steak cuts are often cuts scored by a commercial machine to break meat fibers. At home, you can tenderize your steaks by pounding them with a mallet specially designed for the purpose, or by pounding them lightly in all directions with the blunt side of a knife or side of a plate.

Tenderizing meat with special mallet.

You may choose to use a commercial meat tenderizer on flavorful braising-beef cuts before grilling. Sprinkle the meat lightly and evenly on all sides with either seasoned or unseasoned meat tenderizer. Tenderizer comes in a shaker jar and looks like salt, or it may come in liquid form. Follow directions closely for best results.

In marinades, the vinegar mixed with oil works chemically to make meat more tender. The meat is submerged in the marinade for a specific time (usually overnight) so that the meat has time to become tender and soak up the flavor of the marinade. Marinating for longer than a couple of hours should be done in the refrigerator; for less time, at room temperature.

One handy way to marinate meat is to place the meat in a Ziploc bag, pour the marinade into the bag over the meat, seal the bag, then place in a bowl (be sure that the marinade completely covers the meat) in your refrigerator. Turn bag at least three to four times. One advantage of bags is you don't need to use as much marinade. A good habit is to turn the meat whenever you open your refrigerator.

Italian dressing makes an easy-to-use, spicy marinade that gives meat a distinctive flavor as it tenderizes. You can use the bottled or powdered dressings, or you can make it yourself with oil, vinegar, and seasoning.

Recipes for Grill Cooking

These recipes will appeal to the most discriminating as well as to the heartiest eaters in your crowd.

Unbelievable Flank Steak

Unbelievably delicious!

2–3 pounds flank steak	2 tablespoons vinegar
¾ cup vegetable oil	1 tablespoon powdered garlic
¼ cup soy sauce	½ teaspoon ginger
3 tablespoons honey	6 green onions, chopped

Sprinkle water on both sides of steak. Combine remaining ingredients in a medium-sized bowl for marinade. Place steak in large Ziploc bag, then pour in marinade to cover. Seal bag and refrigerate for 2 hours or overnight. Remove steak from marinade and grill 15 to 20 minutes; turning often. Remove steak from grill, and cut into thin slices on the diagonal, across the grain of the meat.

Yield: 4–6 servings

Steak on the Rocks

This is a real show stealer.

For steak on the rocks, the following beef cuts are best to use—cut ¾-inch to 1-inch thick—T-bone, porterhouse, round steak, sirloin, club, boneless loin, flank steaks, small roasts.

Start a hardwood fire so that it burns down to a bed of coals. You will need a bed of coals at least two inches deep in an area about one-third larger than the total area of the steaks you plan to cook. Be sure to burn all the wood needed for your coals at the same time. You can't add wood later because it will still be flaming when you are ready to cook. While the fire is burning down to a bed of coals, prepare the meat.

Trim the fat off each piece to avoid flare-ups. Steaks should be about the size of your hand for easiest handling. Score the edges of the steaks every inch or so to allow meat to lay flat.

Don't add salt or seasonings or sauces until after the meat is cooked. Salt draws juices out and tomato and barbecue sauces will burn.

When the hardwood fire is burned down to a bed of large coals, spread the coals out to form a flat three-inch bed big enough to place the meat on. Knock the top coals to make sure all of the ash has been removed. With steak in hand, hold your breath, be brave, and place that beautiful steak directly on the coals. Then stand back and watch it cook. It won't take long, perhaps 3 to 4 minutes, for the first side.

Steak cooking directly on coals.

When the steak is ready, turn it with long-handled tongs. Flick off any coals or ash that have stuck to the surface, and cook the other side for a little shorter time, because the meat is already hot. When done, remove from the fire, season, and serve. You may want to use the following sauce on your steak.

Mushroom Sauce

Great topping for any steak.

4 tablespoons flour
4 tablespoons butter or
  margarine
1 10½-ounce can condensed
  beef consomme plus water
  to equal 2 cups.

1 3–4-ounce can of
  mushrooms, drained and
  chopped
Salt and pepper to taste

Blend flour and butter thoroughly in pan. Stir in consomme and water. Cook, stirring constantly, until the sauce thickens, then add mushrooms. Season with salt and pepper.

Marinated Beef Round

Succulent steak!

1 4-pound round steak or
  round roast
1 cup grape juice
⅓ cup red wine vinegar
  with garlic
1 cup onion, chopped

2 tablespoons instant beef
  boullion powder
1 package Italian salad
  dressing mix
¼ cup chopped parsley

Pierce meat deeply with a fork so that flavors will penetrate better. Place in Ziploc bag in a large bowl. Combine other ingredients in the bag and seal. Marinate in refrigerator 24 to 48 hours, turning occasionally.

Roast over cooking coals, basting every 20 minutes for 1½ hours, or until thermometer inserted into thickest part of meat registers 140 degrees F. for rare. Longer time is required for a medium or well-done roast.

Yield: 6–8 servings

Teriyaki Roll-Ups

1 pound top round steak
½ pound bacon
½ cup soy sauce
3 tablespoons sesame oil

¼ cup brown sugar
1 teaspoon ground ginger
2 cloves garlic, minced
¼ teaspoon pepper

Thinly slice round steak across grain, about ⅛-inch thick. Lay out strips of bacon, stretching them as long as they will go. Place strips of meat on bacon and roll. Secure with toothpicks. Mix soy sauce, brown sugar, oil and spices. Marinate meat rolls in soy sauce mixture 4–6 hours in refrigerator. Grill until steak and bacon are done. Serve as appetizers or entrée with oriental food.

Yield: 4 servings

Barbecued Ribs

Utterly delicious!

Beef ribs (allow ¾ to 1
    pound per person)
1 onion

1 bay leaf
Salt to taste
1 peppercorn

In a large kettle, cover ribs with cold water. Add onion and spices and bring to a boil. Cover and simmer for one hour or until meat is tender. Drain and chill until ready to grill. Place ribs on grill. Baste with barbecue sauce. Turn often on grill, basting each time you turn. Grill for about 10 to 15 minutes.

For barbecue sauce, the commercial bottled sauce is good. It's thick and has a great flavor. But for a homemade sauce that is mellower in flavor and lets through the meat taste, try the following:

1 8-ounce can tomato sauce	2 tablespoons prepared
¼ cup molasses	mustard
2 tablespoons vinegar	½ teaspoon salt
	⅛ teaspoon ground cloves

Mix all ingredients well in a bowl.

Yield: 1½ cups of sauce, enough for five pounds of ribs

Grilled Hamburger Specialties

A tasty change from ordinary hamburgers.

1 pound ground beef	¼ teaspoon salt
1 egg	¼ cup minced onion
½ teaspoon monosodium	¼ cup fresh or canned
glutamate (Accent)	tomatoes, seeded,
½ teaspoon nutmeg	peeled, chopped

Topping

¼ cup chopped onion	¾ cup sour cream
2 tablespoons butter	

Mix together ground beef, egg, monosodium glutamate, nutmeg, salt, onion, and tomato. Form into four patties. Arrange on grill that is five inches from hot coals; for medium rare, grill 5 minutes on each side.

For topping: Sauté onions in butter in small skillet at edge of grill. To serve, top with a spoonful of onion and butter mixture and with a spoonful of sour cream.

Yield: 4 servings

Guacamole Burgers

You won't be able to get enough!

3 pounds hamburger
3 avocados, mashed
½ cup onion, finely diced
½ medium-sized tomato, diced

1 teaspoon salt
Pinch of pepper
1 tablespoon Worcestershire
sauce

Press hamburger into patties and season to taste. Combine mashed avocados with the remaining ingredients. Grill hamburgers. When finished cooking, place avocado mixture on burgers and serve.

Yield: 12 burgers

Peachy Burger

A peach of a dish!

1 pound ground beef
¼ cup chopped nuts
1 small onion, grated
1 teaspoon salt

⅛ teaspoon each: cloves,
ginger, pepper
1 4-ounce jar baby food
strained peaches

Glaze

1 tablespoon brown sugar
2 teaspoons vinegar

⅛ teaspoon ginger

Combine ground beef with chopped nuts, grated onion, salt, spices, and 3 tablespoons of the strained peaches. Mix and form into four patties. Grill over glowing coals 3–4 minutes, then brush with glaze of remaining strained peaches that have been seasoned with the sugar, vinegar, and ginger. Turn the patties, brush again, and grill 3–4 minutes longer.

Yield: 4 servings

Inside-Out Hamburger

Better than any fast foods treat!

2 pounds ground beef	2 large sliced onions
½ pound sliced cheese	Heavy-duty foil
4 pickles, chopped	

Season ground beef with salt and pepper (or use ground-beef mixture from stuffing-burger recipe). Portion out beef with rolling pin. Roll out into 12 or 14 large round thin patties. On a piece of heavy-duty foil approximately 12-by-18 inches, place two slices of onion, and one beef patty. In the center of the patty place grated cheese and chopped pickles. Leave about ½-inch space on the outside edge of the meat patty. Place another patty over the cheese and pickles and gently press the meat together around the edges. Place two more onion slices over the combination and wrap using the drugstore wrap. Continue until all patties are used. Place on coals for 12 minutes per side or until done.

For variety you may want to try other vegetables inside of the hamburger, such as chopped tomatoes, mushrooms, zucchini, green peppers, grated cheese, barbecue sauce, relish, crumbled blue cheese with fresh parley, chili, chopped onions and grated cheese, or any other creative and imaginative fillings that also add taste. Almost anything that can be cooked with meat will taste good inside your inside-out hamburger.

Yield: 6–7 servings

Stuffing Burgers

An excellent way to extend meat.

1 5-ounce package herb-seasoned stuffing mix	¼ teaspoon pepper
	⅓ cup Parmesan cheese
½ cup milk	8 hamburger buns, split and toasted
2 eggs	
2 pounds ground beef	8 onion rings and 8 tomato slices (optional)
1 teaspoon salt	

Combine stuffing mix and milk; let stand until all stuffing mix is moistened. Add ground beef, egg, salt, pepper and Parmesan cheese; mix well. Shape into eight patties. Grill for approximately 12 minutes per side. Place on toasted bun halves and top with onion rings and tomato slices, if desired.

Yield: 8 servings

Fish on a Grill

A delicacy.

1 fish steak or fillet	1 tablespoon fresh parsley, chopped
2 tablespoons cooking oil	
1 tablespoon butter	2 lemon wedges, each ⅙ of a lemon

Handling fish carefully, brush it with oil and place fish on grill. Brush with oil again before turning it. Before removing from grill, squeeze lemon juice onto fish so the lemon will simmer into fish. Cook only until fish has lost translucent look and flakes easily: 1½-inch fish steaks, 4 to 6 minutes each side; small fish fillets or ½-inch steaks, 3 to

4 minutes each side; large fish, 10 to 12 minutes each side.
Serve with melted butter, chopped parsley, and lemon wedge.
Yield: One fish, per serving. If
small fillets, allow two per serving.

Cherry-Glazed Ham

A better-than-ever way to serve ham!

8 ham slices, ¼-inch thick   1 21-ounce can cherry pie
filling

Grill the ham over hot coals until hot. Place ham on
plates, then pour two tablespoons warmed cherry-pie filling in the center of each slice, spreading to the corners of
the ham.

Yield: 8 servings

Cherry-glazed ham.

Stuffed pork chops.

Grilled Stuffed Pork Chops

Chops flavored for a feast.

Have the butcher prepare the pork chops by slicing extra-thick chops part way through to create a pocket in each. Or if you are skilled enough and have a sharp knife, you can do it yourself. Partially frozen chops are easiest to cut.

Precook your own favorite stuffing or use a commercial stuffing by following directions on the package and adding nuts, mushroom, etc. Open up the pocket of meat and fill with the stuffing, packing it in lightly. If the stuffing tends to fall out because you are overgenerous, secure the chop by skewering toothpicks through the meat.

Caution: Be sure to cook pork when your charcoal has stopped burning with intense heat, or place the meat to one side of the hottest part of your fire so that the outside won't burn before the inside cooks. Pork must be thoroughly cooked. Turn frequently. It takes at least 20 to 30 minutes to cook chops completely.

117

For variety, you can fill the pocket of your pork chops with many foods other than stuffing. Cheeses are good, especially blue cheese or Swiss. Try chili or a thick paste made up of a barbecue sauce thickened with Parmesan cheese and chopped mushrooms. You may want to combine the barbecue sauce–Parmesan cheese mixture with pineapple chunks or a piece of sliced pineapple.

Sizzling Franks

A hit with young and old.

Cut a narrow lengthwise slit in the frankfurters. Do not cut completely through. Fill with chosen filling, then wrap strip of bacon tightly around each frank, covering slit completely. Secure with toothpicks. Cook on grill until bacon is crisp on all sides. If desired, baste with barbecue sauce.

Suggested fillings:

1. 1 cup shredded cheddar cheese, ½ cup crushed corn chips, ¼ cup taco or barbecue sauce
2. Strips of cheese with strips of dill pickle
3. Sweet pickle relish
4. Finely chopped onion
5. Crushed pineapple
6. Crumbled blue cheese and chopped parsley
7. Kidney beans, tomato sauce, finely chopped onion, and grated cheese
8. Cheese with tomato chunks and diced mushrooms
9. Chili sauce
10. Pineapple and pimento cheese spreads
11. Pork 'n beans
12. Chili with cheese
13. Cheese, crushed pineapple, and minced green pepper

Allow one or two franks per serving. For parties, you may want to set out bacon, franks, and fillings, then allow each guest to create his own sizzling franks.

Popsicle Hot Dogs

Fun and easy to serve for children.

10 frankfurters	10 hot dog buns
10 popsicle sticks	Relish, mustard, catsup

Push popsicle stick into end of frank, leaving 2½ to 3 inches of stick exposed. Sticks make wieners easy to turn on the grill. Serve hot franks on buns with relish, mustard, and other favorites.

Yield: 10 servings

Taco Dogs

A new, delicious slant on tacos.

12 hard corn taco shells	1 head iceburg lettuce, shredded
12 frankfurters	1 8-ounce bottle hot sauce (you won't use complete bottle)
½ pound cheddar cheese, grated	
4 tomatoes, chopped	

Grill the franks. Place each frank in taco shell; add grated cheese, tomatoes and lettuce and top with hot sauce to taste.

Yield: 12 tacos

For variety, use soft corn or flour tortillas, or pita bread. You can also add baked beans or chili.

Taco dogs.

Tater dogs.

Tater Dogs

A great hors d'oeuvre.

1 2-pound package Tater Tots	1 pound sliced bacon, cut to size

Thaw Tater Tots. Roll Tater Tot in a piece of bacon. Cut off excess bacon and secure with a toothpick. Repeat until Tater Tots are covered. Place on a grill to cook. Turn frequently until Tater Tots are done and bacon is cooked and crisp.

Yield: about 24–30 hors d'oeuvres

Date Appetizer

Yummy!

24 dates, pitted
½ pound cheddar cheese,
   grated

12 strips bacon, halved

Fill dates with cheese. Wrap ½ slice of bacon around date and secure with toothpick. Grill until bacon is crisp.

Yield: 24 hors d'oeuvres

Stir-Fry Zucchini

A taste great for zucchini lovers.

Vegetable oil or drippings
   from bacon or steak
1 small zucchini, cut in
   ¼-inch slices

4 medium fresh mushrooms,
   sliced
Salt to taste
½ teaspoon thyme
½ teaspoon rosemary

Cover bottom of flat grill with oil or meat drippings. Heat grill until it begins to smoke. Add zucchini and cook 4 minutes, stirring constantly. Do not overcook zucchini. It should be just tender. Add spices, salt, and pepper to taste.

Yield: 4 servings

Donut S'more Delights

Dessert or snacks—delicious!

1 dozen cake doughnuts
1 6-ounce package milk
   chocolate chips

7-ounce jar marshmallow
   cream
1–2 bananas, sliced

Cut doughnuts in half horizontally. Embed milk chocolate chips on one half, spread marshmallow cream and banana slices on the other half. Grill over low heat until chocolate chips and marshmallow cream begin to melt. Put the halves together for a super dessert.

Yield: 12 servings

6. Backyard Family Fun

Your most rewarding backyard experiences can be with those who find your backyard their native habitat—your family. Why not take some time to enjoy each other as a family as you share backyard activities? Who knows? Outdoor activities may be that dash of spice that turns brothers, sisters, and parents into best friends. Some families have found it worthwhile to set apart one evening a week to spend together. Such evenings of fun, food, and family sharing provide a pleasant break from work, school, and home routines that often make members of the family relative strangers.

Planning family activities together.

Eating fun: a backward dinner.

Assign a chairperson for each special family evening, and by all means encourage children to join in the planning and organizing, along with Mom and Dad. The chairperson can be in charge of organizing a favorite backyard activity, planning a memorable meal to cook out-of-doors (coordinating with an adult), and generally creating enthusiasm for the upcoming "family night." Be sure to keep activities geared to the whole family. And the more people you involve in planning, preparation, and cooking, the more fun the evening will be. Invite friends or perhaps another family to join you if you like. The important thing is for all to relax and enjoy themselves.

Family Outdoor Mealtime Fun

These interesting twists will make a backyard mealtime even more fun for your family.

Backward Dinner

Try a meal with a slightly unorthodox flavor—start at the end and finish at the beginning. Eat your dessert first, then the main course, then, for the finale, end with the blessing of the food. You may wish to try eating left-handed, if you're normally right-handed, or vice versa. Or you may decide to wear your clothes backwards for the event. "Thank yous" and "pleases" can be switched when passing the food. ("Thank you, pass the carrots.") Do whatever is fun, but backwards.

One-Dollar Dinner

This one involves the whole family, and takes the load of planning the dinner off Mom or Dad. Plan for the family to visit the local grocery store together. Give each member of the family one dollar (or another predetermined amount—whatever is realistic). Each person may spend that money on whatever he or she wants the family to eat. Result: You'll have a potpourri dinner. Set a few guiding rules. For example, each person should keep within the money limit and must buy enough of each item for the entire family. Set a time limit—perhaps fifteen minutes—for shopping. Fifteen minutes should also be allowed for preparation time. You may choose to eliminate junk food. Each person must prepare the item he or she purchases.

Not only will you come up with a relatively inexpensive dinner, but watch the creativity start flowing in your family. Who knows what lavish grill or shish kebab creations you may end up with for dinner! And if the end result is tasty, you've had your fun and eaten it, too.

Good-Sport Meal

This novel approach to leftovers makes a memorable "instant picnic." One family member cleans out the leftovers from the fridge, heats and serves them on individual plates, and assigns each plate a number. Then each member of the family draws a number that corresponds to the dishes. The chairperson enthusiastically delivers the matching dish to the appropriate good sport.

Meal on a Blackboard

Here's a way to involve the entire family in preparing an outdoor meal and a great way to handle Sunday dinner. Early in the morning, Mom or Dad outlines the evening's meal on a chalkboard or poster, listing an assignment for each member of the family. Included in each assignment are such details as preparation time for fire, coals, or food, and when each assignment should be finished.

Then, as the family members wake up in the morning, each signs up for the task of his or her choice. Assignments are made on a first-come, first-served basis, thus providing extra incentive for family members to get up early. And for those who don't follow through—clean-up and dish duty!

Another variation of the blackboard dinner: Hold a morning lottery. Early in the morning, perhaps at the breakfast table, have each family member draw an assignment from a hat.

Balcony Picnic

Apartment dwellers will enjoy special family outdoor dinners on a balcony or the roof. You can add fun to your picnic by letting each family member cook his own food on his own flowerpot grill (see p. 29). Offer a light summer meal such as hamburgers, popsickle hot dogs, or shish kebab served with fruit salad; and perhaps a special dessert, such as cake-filled oranges. For family after-dinner activities, stretch your creativity to adapt your favorite games or sports to limited space. For instance, play "basketball" using a Ping-Pong ball and a waste basket.

Leaf-Rakers' Fall Fling

Fall's crisp days inspire hearty outdoor cooking. After your family has spent a Saturday afternoon raking leaves (and reraking them after the kids have played at making leaf forts, etc.) and readying house and garden for the coming winter, you could reward that hard work with a hearty outdoor meal of hamburgers, chili, or other food. If you've spent the afternoon working with the family, these fix-ahead entrées may come in handy:

Thermos Chili Dogs: Tie string or dental floss to a warmed frankfurter, then stick it into a Thermos full of hot chili (as an alternative, use your favorite soup), making sure the string dangles outside the Thermos. When you're ready to eat, pull the string to lift the frank out of the Thermos and serve on a bun with the hot chili (or eat with your hot soup).

Tacos in a Bag: Fill a Thermos with your favorite taco filling (precooked hamburger-onions mixed with a can of chili con carne makes a good one). When you're ready to eat, open the top of a bag of corn chips and pour the taco filling over the chips, then eat right out of the bag.

"Chili dog" treat
at autumn party.

Theme Dinners

What better way to brighten up an outdoor meal than to center the meal around a theme—perhaps an interesting foreign country, a holiday, a birthday, or even an "un-birthday" for everyone. Announce the theme for the dinner at the activity night the week before, so the family can help with research about the country, find props, or simply come up with inventive ideas for the celebration.

Taco in a bag.

For example, if you choose the country Turkey as a theme, you may want to serve some dishes the country is noted for, such as shish kebabs made with specially marinated lamb and Mideastern vegetables. Have one family member research some interesting facts or stories about the country to relate at the meal. Have another draw a picture of the country's flag, or make namecards decorated with the flag. Bring flowers native to the country to the dinner table as the centerpiece. Or invite someone you know from that country to join you for dinner. If you live near a university, you may discover a foreign student who would like to have dinner with an American family. Then center a meal around the country of your guest.

Meals with a holiday theme can be very creative celebrations as well. For example, for Valentine's Day, you may wish to enlist the children in cutting as many food items as possible into heart shapes (such as cheese, hamburger patties, or refrigerator rolls). For April Fool's Day, try something unusual, such as tinting the food an unexpected color. Anyone who has had purple potatoes or green milk will remember that meal for quite a while!

For birthdays or anniversaries, let the person or couple to be honored select favorite foods for your outdoor dinner. You may even want to have an awards night to celebrate that person or couple, with family members creating awards in a serious or humorous way.

Backyard Fun and Games

One garnish to a good outdoor meal is the laughter, warmth, and fun of games and activities families and friends can enjoy together. Here are a few suggestions.

Tape-Recorder Scavenger Hunt

Try a new approach to scavenging—hunt for sounds! Divide your family into at least two groups, each armed with a portable tape recorder. (Many public libraries will check out cassette recorders, or perhaps you can borrow them from friends and neighbors.) Be sure each tape recorder has good batteries. Test before using it.

Each group should be given the same list of about fifteen outdoor sounds to find, with points assigned for each sound.

Taping scavenger-hunt sounds.

Select from the list below some sounds that can be heard in your neighborhood. Assign points according to difficulty. For example:

10 Points	5 Points	2 Points
Tumbling stream	Horn honking	Engine running
Singing bird	Neighbor's dog	Clanging garbage
Plane passing	barking	can lid
overhead	Song by team	Crackling of a
Thunder	member	twig
Police siren	Purring cat	Running water
Animal sound	Skateboarding	
	sound	

Each group has 30 minutes (or whatever time limit may be set) to find and record as many of the sounds as possible and then return to the home base. At the end of the assigned time, each group can compare tapes and compute scores for the winner.

Family Olympics

Create your own peculiar brand of the Olympics in your backyard using easily obtained household items. Have a record keeper note each person's feats. Handicap points may be assigned to equalize competition among family members, as the case may be.

Discus Throw. Using a paper plate as a discus, see who can throw it the farthest. (Be sure to use Olympic form.)

Shot Put. Have someone demonstrate shot-put form. Then have each member take three tries at throwing a balloon that's been blown up. (You may wish to substitute a paper bag that has been blown up and tied if you don't have any balloons around the house.)

Throwing the "discus" in the family Olympics.

A real high jump—family Olympics style.

Handicap race.

High Jump. Family members serve as posts holding high jump string "hurdle." Be sure to hold string loosely to prevent injury.

Javelin Throw. Again, someone may wish to demonstrate Olympic form. Each family member takes turns to see how far he or she can throw a straw.

Fifty-Yard Dash. Have all family members come to a starting line, each holding a spoon with a cotton ball in it. The first person who runs to a predetermined spot and back across the starting line without losing the cotton ball is the winner.

Handicap Race. Place a large piece of plastic or a poncho on the ground. Along one side place a cotton ball for each member of the family. At a given signal, each person begins to blow his or her cotton ball across the plastic to the other side. The first one to blow the cotton off the opposite edge is the winner.

Relay. Pair off the family members, and give each pair two ten-inch cardboard squares. One person in each set will hop from square to square as his or her partner places the squares in front of him or her. After covering a set distance, the two teammates then switch roles and scramble back to the starting line. If a "runner" lands anywhere but on a cardboard square, he or she must begin again.

Use your imagination on how to reward the winners of each event. Be sure that everyone in the family "wins" something and feels important.

Pioneer Party

Easterners and Westerners alike will enjoy reliving the days when the '49ers crossed the plains. Try creating an authentic pioneer meal, cooking over a wood fire, and using utensils and ingredients that a nineteenth-century pioneer would have had on hand. With a little research and some

Backyard pioneers.

ingenuity, you'll come up with games, costumes, food, and activities that your family and friends will remember for a long time—and maybe improve your youngsters' history grades in the process.

- Recipes. Find out what kinds of food the pioneers ate, and prepare that food for your outdoor meal. A typical menu might look like this:

Buffalo (or Beef) Stew
Sourdough Muffins or Johnny Cakes (Cornmeal Biscuits)
Green Salad with Dairy Salad Dressing
Honey or Molasses Candy or Wild Berry Cobbler
Apple Cider and Raw Milk

- Stories. If family members know any pioneer stories, ask them to share them with the rest of the family. Ideally, you may have some stories of your own ancestors. You may even have a family member or two reenact some experience.
- Games. Play games such as charades, forfeits, and others that pioneer adults and children enjoyed.
- Dance. You may want to end your activity with a genuine square dance, with a recorded or live "caller."

Penny Walk

For a serendipitous excursion, walk with the family to the nearest corner, flip a penny, and if it lands heads, go left; tails, go right. Keep walking until you get tired—then head home for delicious refreshments cooked on your grill.

Magazine Scavenger Hunt

This can be done out on the patio on a warm summer evening. Give each member of the family a stack of old magazines, a pair of scissors, and a list of ten specific items—such as a black dog, a dessert with whipped cream on top, a woman wearing gold earrings. Lists can be identical or different, but make sure all the lists contain items that are equally easy or difficult to find. The first person to find all the pictures on his or her list wins.

Collage Decorating

Old magazines are recycled in this activity, too. Have each member of the family choose a subject of personal interest: animals, flowers, airplanes, sports cars, movie stars—whatever is appealing. Then each person can cut pictures on his or her theme from the magazines and glue them to a large piece of butcher paper. Shellac them. When dry, hang on walls in the house. You may even wish to frame them. Or glue the magazine cutouts to an empty five-gallon ice cream carton (usually available free at an ice cream shop), shellac the collage, and use the finished product as a wastepaper basket. For a finishing touch, trim the basket with lace or narrow leather strips.

Treasure Hunt

Give each family member a slip of paper with a clue on it. This leads to other clues hidden throughout the yard. The last clue should lead to the treasure: a favorite dessert, game, or some other prize.

Activities to Strengthen Family Ties

After a good outdoor meal, these activities will generate those warm family feelings and make them last for days to come.

Family Member of the Night

Take the time, apart from birthdays, to honor each member of the family. Perhaps have one member of the family do a mock radio interview with the honored person, using the tape recorder to document that person's favorite things, happiest moments of the year, year in school, and progress made during the year. You can also display his or her picture. Have each family member write something special about that person. The picture and comments can be placed on a bulletin board honoring the family-member-

Honoring family-member-of-the-night.

of-the-week. You will find your children looking forward to their turns. This is a great morale builder and an opportunity to give positive feedback to family members. It's also a good time to serve the honored person's favorite foods and join in his or her favorite activity.

Treasure Box

One evening while you're enjoying the backyard, consider making a family treasure box or individual treasure boxes. Cover a milk crate or comparable cardboard or wooden box with contact paper; or if you are making individual

A treasure box
for saving special
mementos.

treasure boxes, let each person select his or her favorite contact paper at the local market. The box will then serve to contain one's "treasures" and personal papers. For a child about to start school, it's a good idea to provide large envelopes marked "first grade," "second grade," "third grade," and on through the grades. At the end of each year the youngster can select special papers to place in the appropriate envelope.

You may also want to take a tape recorder into the backyard and let family members tape their feelings and impressions of special occasions, family vacations, and other things that are special to them. Each year, add to the tape and make the tape a part of the treasure box. The box is also a great place to keep news clippings of family members and current events. It's a handy and unique way to keep a record of treasured moments and accomplishments.

Family Photo Night

After a memorable outdoor meal, a stroll down memory lane may be fun, especially if Mom and Dad pull out the pictures of themselves when they were young. Take a look at slides or movies of family members when they were younger, and have Mom and Dad (or perhaps an older brother or sister) tell stories about each child when they were younger.

For a particularly valuable evening, ask Grandma and Grandpa to bring their family photos to your outdoor meal, then tape them as they tell about each photo. Your family tree will come alive for you and your children as Grandma tells about her family, graduation day, and other special events in the photos. You may even wish to construct a real "family tree," drawn on butcher paper taped to the patio supports or the side of the house.

You may want to set a particular time of the year to have an annual outdoor family photo session. One family snaps a new family portrait in the backyard each winter. With the idea of using these portraits as Christmas-tree ornaments, they are set in small frames (a large jar lid that has been decorated works well). These unique ornaments form a fascinating family history.

Awareness Night

Choose an evening to simulate a handicap in every family member: Blindfold one, give one ear plugs, have one hold up one foot and use crutches, and let another wear his or her writing arm in a sling. Have the family prepare the meal and clean up, each working around the handicap. All members should be aware of each other's handicaps and help each other whenever possible. After cleanup sit down and have each member tell what his or her particular handicap was like. How did it feel to *help* the handicapped? What did you learn about the feelings of handicapped people? Children—and parents—can learn to develop a more acute awareness of the needs of a physically handicapped person and a greater appreciation for their own abilities to see, hear, and walk—priceless gifts we seldom appreciate until they are lost. This is an excellent activity to help members of the family develop empathy for others.

Spotlight on Parents

What was life like when Mom and Dad were children? How did they live, and where? What are some of their fondest memories? What was life like without television? What was school like? Let the kids interview Mom and Dad (on a tape to be saved in the family archives) about their early lives, what they thought and did, how they met, etc. The next week, the kids may wish to stage a "This Is Your Life" for their parents.

Instead of (or along with) Mom and Dad, you may want to dedicate an evening to Grandpa and Grandma. Tapes or cassettes of their memories, whether they live down the block or across the continent, will become a family treasure.

Family Service Night

Decide to help someone in your community. You may know an elderly person in your neighborhood who could use some help with painting, mowing the lawn, or weeding the garden. Tactfully arrange beforehand to render the help. If you don't know someone, you may wish to "adopt" a friend at a rest home and visit that person at least once a month as a family, bringing extra "banana boats" you've cooked, cards at holidays, or little items that the person may need. You may even consider taking that person for a ride or outing occasionally or invite them to family night in the backyard.

You may wish to "pixilate" another family in your neighborhood by doing anonymous good deeds for them. Try getting up early and clearing their walks if it's snowy outside, taking care that they don't see you; or drop off barbecued chicken and other goodies on their doorstep. Perhaps you could spend a few minutes at the dinner table coming up with new ideas for pixilating a family.

Neighborhood potluck cookouts or an exchange of outdoor meal nights with another family are great fun. Share your favorite outdoor meal one week with them, and they can share their favorite outdoor dishes with you the next week.

Playing pixie—
leaving treats on
a neighbor's doorstep.

A good way to encourage budding stars is to present an evening of family talents to top off your backyard meal. Have everyone prepare at least one number, whether singing, dancing, playing the guitar or piano, pantomiming, telling a story, or doing impressions. Make sure that the performances are scheduled by the middle of the previous week to allow proper rehearsal time. Assign one person to be emcee for the newsworthy event. And, of course, reward the participants with delicious refreshment.

Backyard Family Campout

Sleeping under starry skies, eating food cooked over glowing coals, telling ghost stories in the dark, enjoying your family in the outdoors—these camping pleasures can be yours in your own backyard. Instead of spending money and precious vacation time to travel to a camping spot, why not camp out at home?

Family backyard
camp-out.

A backyard campout offers a refreshing activity for families with young children who would like to go camping, for parents who want to vacation with their family but cannot take time from work, for grandparents whose many grandchildren descend upon them at reunion time, and for families who have one or more members who aren't convinced that roughing it in the wilds is fun. A backyard campout is also an excellent time to teach new outdoor skills to would-be campers, to test new camping equipment and techniques, or to serve as a short dry run for a major family camping trip.

Plan your backyard campout as carefully as you would plan any other camping trip: plan your menus, gather the food and equipment you'll need, and assign responsibilities for cooking, fire duty, activities, and cleanup to various family members.

You can sleep in sleeping bags or pitch a tent in the backyard; cook all of your meals outdoors or eat picnic style; and fill your weekend with family outdoor fun.

If you want to eliminate trips to the house for dressing for sprinkler or swimming-pool fun or putting on pajamas, construct this instant dressing room, using a large, sturdy umbrella with a hooked handle, a shower curtain, and a handy tree branch. Open the umbrella and suspend it from a tree branch so that the umbrella hangs about six feet from the ground. Slip the holes at the top of the shower curtain over the ends of the protruding umbrella ribs, so that the curtain forms a dressing room around the umbrella (overlap at least two holes to form a "door").

One source of endless fun is to fill a waterbed out on the lawn. Children can jump, bounce, and generally have a good time on it. You'll need to move it every two or three days, however, or relocate it in a spot where it won't kill the lawn.

Umbrella dressing room for backyard privacy.

Additional Activities

We've presented a few ideas for getting the family together and having some outdoor fun in the backyard. There are, of course, many other activities you can devise. A little imagination, a lot of enthusiasm, and your own great ideas will create memorable outdoor fun with your family and friends.

And don't forget some of the more traditional outdoor activities: bike riding together, visiting a nearby state park, fishing, a family slumber party out-of-doors, a cook-out at the beach, horseback riding, a moonlight swim, a harbor cruise (if you're close to water), building a snowman, or planting a garden, with each child in charge of the upkeep in a particular spot in the garden.

Investing time in your family, rather than money, lasts longer! It's a pure investment that will grow with time—not just ten percent but a hundredfold.

7. Parties and Party Planning Guide

Most people love a party—and what better way is there to enjoy your backyard? Invite your favorite people, do as much as possible in advance, prepare plenty of good food, and you will be sure to have a terrific time. You will need to consider your resources carefully—money, space, and time. And take into consideration which of your friends enjoy each other the most. Then make out the guest list and send off your invitations.

Invitations

You don't need to rely on traditional invitations. Try to come up with something creative that will tickle the imagination of your guests. A few suggestions:

- Mission Impossible. Leave an inexpensive cassette tape recording and a few photos relating to the party (or even pictures from magazines) in the mailbox of the person you are inviting. On the tape, list where the party will be held, when, what to wear, what to bring (if it's potluck), and any other pertinent information. Their mission, should they decide to accept, is to attend the party and cook a particular item on the menu.
- Balloon. Place the invitation inside of a balloon before blowing the balloon up. In order to get the invitation, the guest must pop the balloon. You may wish to leave a note on the balloon string that an important message can be found inside.

Walnut-shell invitation.

Matchbook invitation.

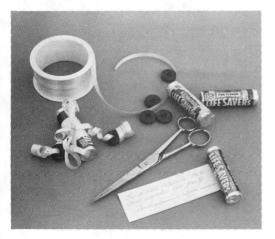
Lifesaver invitation.

Puzzle invitation.

- Walnut Shell. Crack open a walnut, take out the meat, then write a note on a long strip of paper, inviting your friends to join you for an evening of nutty fun. Place the folded note in the shell Chinese-fortune-cookie style. Glue shell back together and deliver to your friends.
- Matchbook. Invite your friends to "light up their lives" by pasting the invitation on the inside of the matchbook.
- Lifesavers. Wrap the invitation around a roll of Lifesavers to invite your "life-saving friends" to the party.

- Puzzle. Write out an invitation, then cut it up in pieces like a puzzle. Place the pieces in an envelope, and mail it to your friends.
- Serial. Make up a hair-raising story about the party and send it out serial form to your intended guests, adding details in each installment that tell them time, place, what to wear, what to bring. End each installment with "To be continued . . ." until all the details for the party have been sent out.
- Ribbons. For a neighborhood party, send a ribbon with each guest's name printed on it with each invitation. Ask your guests to "tie a ribbon on the birch tree by the porch" (or any easy-to-find tree you have) if they can come. Or send a different colored ribbon to each person and keep track of which color belongs to which person, so you will know who's coming when the ribbon appears on your tree.

Menu

The food you serve can add a special flair to a party—especially if it is the kind of food that adds color as well as tastiness. It is smart to choose recipes that can be prepared in advance, so you don't have to cope with last-minute preparation when your guests start arriving. Plan a menu (if it's a dinner party) that can stand a few minutes in case some of your guests arrive late. If you decide to serve an unusually spicy or exotic dish, try to offer a choice of blander dishes in case some guests can't handle the spicy food.

For your own peace of mind, don't attempt to be more elaborate in your food preparation than you can handle. The easier the food is to prepare and serve, the more enjoyable a time you will have.

Choosing Your Kind of Party

There are so many different types of parties you can give—a dinner buffet, potluck, progressive dinner; a party centering around a holiday, such as Thanksgiving, Christmas, or Valentine's Day; parties for no particular occasion, such as an unbirthday party. The party ideas included in this chapter will help you create unusual and fun gatherings.

South Sea Luau

Picture lots of fresh flowers and greenery, mounds of fresh fruits, and enough food to keep even the hungriest guests contented. If you start to smell the roast pork steaming hot from the pit and teriyaki strips on bamboo sticks sizzled to a nice juicy brown, you'll know you are at a luau!

Today Hawaii is considered a luxurious vacation spot. For a really special party, you can turn your backyard into a little Hawaii for a few hours and create a meeting place for your favorite people, even if you can't provide the blue Pacific. A flower centerpiece, flaming torches (actually candles set in sand-filled paper bags), and brightly colored napkins and decorations set the scene. On your invitations, send out the word that muumuus and colorful shirts are the party dress—and be sure to greet your friends with a lei. You or your guests can even make do-it-yourself hula skirts on the spot. Using green crepe paper, measure enough to go around the guest's waist, then make slits in the paper to create the "grass-skirt" effect. Using masking tape as a belt, attach the skirt around the waist. For a thicker "skirt," wrap several layers around the waist. Newspaper can be used instead of crepe paper.

Pick a menu that is typically Hawaiian. You can choose your favorite dishes from the following list:

Kalua Pig (Roast Pig)
Teriyaki Pork Spareribs
Teriyaki Chicken
Teriyaki Meat Sticks
Butter Steamed Fish
Sweet Potatoes (Yams)
Rice
Lomi Lomi Salmon (Fish Salad)
Haupia (Coconut Pudding)
Pineapple Spears
Fruit Salad
Fruit Punch

A suggested menu might include:

Kalua Suckling Pig
Teriyaki Meat Sticks
Yams
Lomi Lomi Salmon
Haupia
Pineapple Spears

Kalua Pig

An essential part of your luau festivities is roasting a suckling pig in a pit. The resulting pork is tender, juicy, and aromatic.

The first step is to dig a pit, or *imu*, for the pig. The size of the pit will depend on the size of your pig, but the pit will need to be big enough to be lined with rocks, too. You will need to gather or acquire about fifty to one hundred pieces

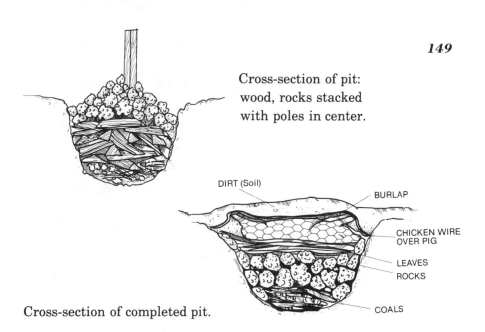

Cross-section of pit:
wood, rocks stacked
with poles in center.

Cross-section of completed pit.

of porous rock (depending on the size of pig) such as lava.
Lava should be about softball size. If you have to use solid
rock, don't use limestone or sandstone. Solid rocks are more
dangerous and could explode, so if you use them don't stand
near the fire while they are heating.

After you have dug the pit, place a pole in the center. The
fire will be built around the pole. Then line the bottom of
the pit with the lava rocks. Form a pyramid of kindling
wood around the pole and stuff plenty of sheets of newspaper that have been tightly crumpled into the pyramid of
kindling. Then stack several rows of quartered logs around
the pyramid and place the rocks on top. Remove the center
pole and drop a match or flaming paper into the hole to
start the fire. Let the fire burn for two to three hours, or
until the rocks are red hot. If any logs are left in the pit,
remove them.

Be sure to order the suckling pig in advance. When you
pick it up, ask the butcher to clean it for you. Also ask the
butcher to slit it open from the throat to the hind quarters
and along joints at top of each leg. (Some people prefer to

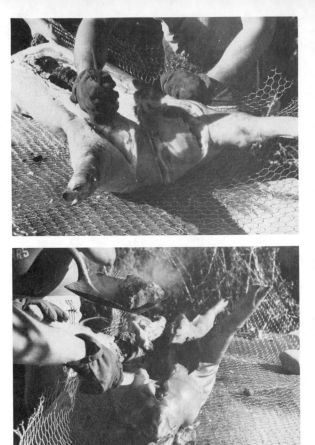

Cutting cavities in pig.

Filling cavities in pig
with hot lava rocks.

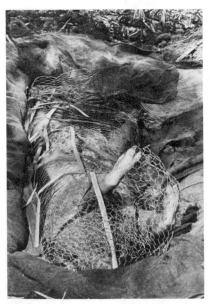

Placing soaked burlap
bags over pit.

Peeling back burlap to expose pigs.

have the pig cut in sections and wrapped in aluminum foil for easier handling.) Just before you are ready to cook it, rub a liberal amount of rock salt in the cavity of the pig, then place about fifteen red-hot medium-sized rocks in the pig's cavity and in slits at top of each leg.

Place cattail stalks or lettuce leaves on the pile of rocks in the pit to keep the pig from direct contact with them. You can usually find cattails along rivers, lakes, or swamps. The pit is now ready for the pig.

To finish preparing the pig, tie all four feet together, then place the pig in chicken wire, wire the top shut, and place it in the pit. If you want to cook anything else in the pit, such as sweet potatoes, chicken, or fish, butter them, wrap them in foil, and place them in the pit now. Acting quickly so that the heat from the rocks doesn't escape, cover everything in the pit with a layer of cattail stalks. Then cover with water-soaked burlap bags overlapping in a circle so that the bags can be peeled back after the pig is cooked. This layer prevents grit from falling on the cooked pig. Soak a tarp (or large piece of cardboard) in water and place it over the burlap bags, then cover everything with dirt, about six inches deep so that no steam can escape from the pit.

The approximate cooking time for the pig should be one hour for every 20 pounds. (It cooks fast in the intense heat of the steam pit.) When the pig is done, carefully remove all the dirt from the pit. Lift the tarp after the dirt has been removed, then peel back the burlap bags carefully so no dirt gets on the food. Remove the rocks from the pig with asbestos gloves or long tongs, and lift the pig from the pit. Remove any other food items from the pit as well. After the pig is taken out of the pit, place it on the table for carving, and put all the meat into serving dishes. Then—enjoy the feast!

Teriyaki
meat sticks.

Teriyaki Sauce

Excellent for any meats you choose to marinate.

1 cup soy sauce
1 cup sugar
½ tablespoon grated ginger root

1 clove crushed garlic
⅓ cup chopped green onions
1 tablespoon sesame-seed oil

Heat soy sauce and sugar until sugar dissolves. **Remove from heat. Add remaining ingredients.**

Teriyaki Meat Sticks

South Sea Oriental delight.

Teriyaki Sauce (see recipe above)

2 pounds sirloin tip steak, sliced ⅛-inch thick

Marinate steak in sauce overnight. Cut steak into strips 1 by 2 inches long. String meat onto bamboo skewers. (If you like, this recipe can be prepared well in advance. Keep meat refrigerated, still in sauce.) Barbecue and eat!

Yield: 6–8 servings

Teriyaki Pork Spareribs

You'll find this sparerib recipe hard to resist.

Make Teriyaki Sauce but substitute 1 cup brown sugar for white sugar.

1 cup pineapple juice or to taste	3 pounds pork spareribs, cut into 3-bone sections
	1 tablespoon oil

Add pineapple juice to Teriyaki Sauce to taste. Set aside. Brown pork spareribs in oil. Drain off oil. Marinate spareribs in sauce overnight, then barbecue and eat.

Yield: 6–8 servings

Teriyaki Steak Sandwich

A South Sea treat with an American look.

8 sirloin tip steaks, sliced ⅛-inch thick	8 hamburger buns
Teriyaki Sauce (recipe above)	Mayonnaise

Marinate steak in Teriyaki Sauce overnight. Barbecue or pan-fry meat. Place in buns spread with mayonnaise. Add lettuce, tomatoes, or onions as desired. Eat!

Yield: 8 servings

Teriyaki Chicken

You have never tasted better chicken.

Teriyaki Sauce (see recipe above)	3½ pounds chicken breasts and thighs

Parboil chicken pieces until almost cooked (approximately 20 minutes). Marinate chicken pieces in Teriyaki Sauce overnight. Arrange on grill over cooking coals and barbecue. Serve with rice, using extra Teriyaki Sauce over the rice.

Yield: 6–8 servings

Baked Sweet Potatoes (Yams)

A good accompaniment to any pork or turkey meal.

8 sweet potatoes   Butter

Wash potatoes and rub with butter, then wrap them in aluminum foil and place on top of the cattails—just before the burlap. Remove from aluminum foil, peel, and cut into one-inch pieces and serve.

Yield: 8 servings

Lomi Lomi Salad

Try this for an interesting salad.

1 pound raw salmon   ½ cup chopped green onion
3 tomatoes   1 tablespoon salt
1 large yellow onion, chopped

Scrape skin from salmon. Chop tomatoes, yellow onion, and green onions. Mix together in a large bowl. Add salt. Mix thoroughly. Chill before eating (it tastes better).

Yield: 6–8 servings

Butter-Steamed Fish

Exceptionally good.

Fish fillet
Salt and pepper to taste
¼ yellow onion, chopped

¼ cup butter
Aluminum foil

Place fish on shiny side of aluminum foil. Salt and pepper, then add onion. Cut butter into squares and place on fish. Seal fish in foil, using drugstore wrap. Cook over coals or in coals. Cook 10 minutes per side.

Sweet and Sour Spareribs

Oriental tastiness at its best.

1 pound spareribs (cut into
    1¼-inch pieces)
2 teaspoons oil
1 clove garlic
1 teaspoon salt

1 teaspoon red *shoyu* (soy
    sauce)
¼ cup vinegar
¼ cup water

Sauce

1 tablespoon cornstarch
1 tablespoon *shoyu* (soy sauce)

1 teaspoon vinegar
2 tablespoons brown sugar

Brown spareribs and garlic in oil. Add salt, then red *shoyu*. Add vinegar and water and simmer until tender, about 20 to 30 minutes. Mix ingredients to make sauce. Add sauce gradually to simmering spareribs. Bring to a boil, and simmer one minute. Serve immediately.

Yield: 4–6 servings

Glazed Sweet Potatoes

Another variation worth trying.

8 sweet potatoes, boiled   1 cup brown sugar
2 tablespoons butter   ½ cup water

Peel boiled sweet potatoes, slice, and arrange in a buttered baking dish. Boil sugar and water in small saucepan for 5 minutes. Pour one third of the syrup over sweet potatoes and bake until brown. Baste with the remaining syrup.

For variety, boil sweet potatoes in thick syrup with butter or with marshmallows on top.

This also makes a delicious dessert.

Yield: 8 servings

Fresh Fruit Salad

Good tasting and pretty, too.

1 cantaloupe   3 pears   1 watermelon
3 oranges   2 bananas
3 apples   1 pineapple

Cut fruit into bite-sized pieces. Place in a hollowed out fluted watermelon. Serve when chilled.

Yield: 8–10 servings

Haupia (Coconut Pudding)

A dessert you won't forget.

2 cups milk   3 tablespoons sugar
14 ounces shredded coconut   Dash of salt
2 tablespoons cornstarch

Heat milk in a saucepan. Pour hot milk over coconut and let stand for 15 to 20 minutes. Strain and squeeze out all liquid (coconut cream), reserve. Combine cornstarch, ½ cup of the coconut cream, sugar, and salt. Stir while adding remaining coconut cream slowly. Cook on low heat, stirring constantly, do not boil. Cook to a smooth consistency. Pour into shallow pan, then chill in refrigerator. When firm, cut into small squares. Serve.

Yield: 6–8 servings

Preparing a Pineapple for a Luau: Buy one large, fresh pineapple that has a full green top. Slice off about 1 to 1½ inches of the pineapple's bottom. Slice off top about 1 to 1½ inches down. With a long, thin, flexible knife, remove the entire contents in one piece from the shell. Cut into 8 spears. Replace the contents in the shell. Garnish with finely chopped mint if desired. Replace bottom and top.

Pineapple Boats

Another delightful way to serve pineapple.

1 fresh pineapple

1 4-ounce bottle maraschino cherries

Cut fresh pineapple in quarters lengthwise without removing crown or outside rind. Leaving rind and crown and core intact, cut under core. Bend grapefruit knife or other curved, flexible blade into a half-moon shape. Cut pineapple close to the rind to detach fruit. Still leaving rind and core intact, remove fruit and cut in slices crosswise. Slip slices back into shell in a staggered arrangement, skewering maraschino cherries to pineapple slices with toothpicks.

Making pineapple boats.

Fruit Punch

A delicious drink for any party.

1 2-quart package
  orange-flavored Kool-Aid
1 2-quart package
  cherry-flavored Kool-Aid
1 6-ounce can frozen orange
  juice concentrate, thawed
2 cups sugar
1½ cups pineapple juice
2 bananas, mashed
Enough water to make one
  gallon of juice
1 quart 7-Up, chilled

Mix Kool-Aid, orange juice, sugar, pineapple juice, and bananas together thoroughly. Add enough cold water to make one gallon of juice. Just before serving, add chilled 7-Up.

This mixture can be frozen in airtight containers and used at a later date, or stored in the refrigerator until needed.

158

Pilgrims' Autumn Feast

Menu

Spit-cooked Turkey
Dressing and Gravy
Baked Potatoes or Yams
Luxury Fruit Liner, Corn on the Cob, or any grilled vegetable
Pumpkin Pie, Ice Cream-Apple Bread Pudding or
Cranberry Ice

Though it may be chilly outdoors, here is one way you can really recreate the Pilgrims' experience that first November in the New World. Using a vertical spit to cook the turkey, you can celebrate Thanksgiving in your backyard. And you can cook the rest of the dinner outdoors, as well! Cooking the turkey is easy: The turkey is hung from a tripod and surrounded by four 2-foot high tubelike chicken-wire cages filled with hot charcoal briquets. Wrap aluminum foil around the charcoal-briquet wire columns, so heat is reflected back to the center where the turkey is hanging. The temperature will vary, depending upon the spacing of the columns of coals and the amount of foil used.

A vertical spit is easy to construct, as you have seen in Chapter 1. You may already have a tripod for cooking, but if you don't, you can form one by tying three straight sticks or pieces of metal piping about 5 feet long and ½ to ¾ inches in diameter together at one end with a wire or string. The turkey is hung by wire from the top of the tripod.

To set up the cooking area, place four 3-foot-high metal rods in a square 24 to 28 inches apart, depending on the size of the turkey. The larger the turkey, the further apart the stakes need to be. If the turkey weighs ten pounds, position the stakes 24 inches apart; if 14 pounds, 26 inches apart, if 16–20 pounds, 28 inches apart. Cut the chicken wire (which will hold the briquets) into 4 pieces about 10 inches across and 2 feet long. Be sure the wire mesh is smaller than the briquets; one-inch mesh works best. Fasten the two long sides of wire together to form tubelike wire cages. Slip a wire cage over each stake.

Fill the bottom half of each wire cage with charcoal briquets that have been "marinated" overnight in a charcoal-starter fluid. Fill the rest of the cage with dry briquets, interspersing a few marinated briquets among them. Then stand back and carefully light them with a match. A few briquets should be added to the wire cages every hour to maintain a constant temperature.

Prepare the bird ahead of time, just as if you were cooking it in the oven. If you stuff your turkey, make sure cooking temperature does not fall below 300 degrees F. to avoid bacterial poisoning. To keep the wings from overcooking, tie a string around the turkey to hold the wings close to the body; and wire the legs together.

To hang the turkey, use about six or seven feet of wire, double and twist together at the end. Loop the wire around the wire holding the turkey's legs together. Slip a Brown-in-Bag over the turkey, and tie it loosely at the top. The bag will keep ashes off the turkey and retain the juices for gravy. Hook the bird to the tripod with the wire you've attached, and adjust the bird so it is six to eight inches off the ground. An inexpensive oven thermometer can be hung by a wire from the tripod at the same level as the turkey to help you determine the temperature inside the vertical spit.

To help maintain the proper temperature, wrap heavy-duty aluminum foil around the four stakes to form a boxlike enclosure. Slide the aluminum up and down to regulate the temperature. If the temperature becomes too hot, slide the

Briquets in wire "cages."

Turkey attached to tripod with potatoes on grill.

Wrapping foil around stakes to form enclosure.

foil up several inches above the ground to allow more circulation for the air. Lower the foil to raise the temperature. Try to maintain a temperature of about 300 to 350 degrees F. Allow 15 to 20 minutes per pound of turkey, and an extra half hour to one hour for the whole turkey if you stuff it. When the turkey is browned to your satisfaction, wrap aluminum foil around it. The foil may add another half hour or so to your cooking time, but it stops the browning. Some turkeys have a gauge that pops out when the turkey is done.

If you plan to add potatoes and yams to your outdoor Thanksgiving feast, prepare them before you start cooking the turkey. Place a sheet of aluminum foil on the ground. On top of it place three rocks or bricks about three to four inches high. Then place a wire rack on top of the rocks. Coat the potatoes and yams with butter, and wrap individually in foil. One and one-half hours before the turkey is done, place briquets on the foil under the rack, spacing them 1½ to 2 inches apart. Place the food on the rack to cook. Bread pudding is delicious with this meal and can be cooked right along with the yams and potatoes.

If you want a pumpkin pie to top off the dinner, plan to cook it in a Dutch oven. Place three small rocks in the bottom of the 12-inch Dutch oven, then place the pie on the rocks to cook. Cover and place the oven over red-hot briquets arranged to form a checkerboard pattern, with briquets about 1½ inches apart. Place briquets on the lid of Dutch oven in the same pattern. Cooking time is about the same as for your indoor oven. Schedule the pie so it is done at the same time as the turkey.

When the turkey is done, take it down and let it cool for a few minutes in the bag. Then gently ease it out of the bag, making sure to save the juices if you want to spoon them over potatoes or make gravy with them. Spoon the stuffing

Pie baked in Dutch oven over briquets 1½ inches apart.

out into a bowl, and carve the turkey. Remove the yams and potatoes from the grill, and take the pie out of the Dutch oven.

Gravy for Turkey

Remove the rocks from the bottom of the Dutch oven and wipe out pot. Pour the juices from the turkey into it. Skim off the excess fat. If there is not enough turkey juice, add water for the amount of gravy desired. Add 1 to 3 tablespoons of cornstarch (amount varies with size of turkey) to ½ cup of cold water and stir. Add this mixture to juices, then stir, and cook until the gravy boils and thickens.

A lovely decoration for the table for everyone to nibble on while they wait is melon and grapes prepared in this unique way:

Fountain of Grapes

A beautiful way to serve fruits.

1 large honeydew melon   Plums
Grapes, both green and red

Cut small slice from bottom of melon so that it can sit firmly on the table. Beginning at the top, cut down but not through the melon, forming 8 slices. This forms the "basket." Clean out seeds and fill basket cavity with washed fruit, letting some spill out the ribs of the basket like a fountain.

Ice Cream-Apple Bread Pudding

The Pilgrims never had it so good!

¼ loaf French bread
2 tablespoons butter
2 tart apples
Juice from 1 lemon
¼ cup brown sugar

½ teaspoon cinnamon
¼ cup raisins
¼ cup apple cider
½ cup chopped nuts

Cut bread lengthwise in ½-inch slices. Butter both sides and cut into 1-inch cubes. Place in a large mixing bowl. Core, peel, and cut apples into small cubes. Add the lemon juice, sugar, cinnamon, raisins, apple cider, and nuts. Mix. Divide bread pudding in half and place on 12-by-18-inch heavy-duty foil and wrap using the drugstore wrap. Place on wire rack two to three inches above the glowing coals or charcoal, or double wrap with foil, newspapers, and foil and put directly on coals for 20 minutes per side. Unwrap and top with ice cream. Serve immediately.

Yield: 4–6 servings

Cranberry Ice

A light heavenly dessert to top off any holiday meal.

4 cups cranberries
6 cups water
2 cups sugar

Juice of 1 lemon
1 teaspoon grated orange rind

Boil cranberries, 2 cups water, and sugar until berries pop open (about 5 minutes). Strain, and add lemon juice, remaining water, and orange rind. Stir well. Freeze. Keeps for months, but must be removed from freezer 45 minutes before serving.

Yield: 8–12 servings.

Pineapple Turkey Centerpiece

For a great centerpiece to top the day, you can't beat a pineapple turkey.

¼ yard red felt
Yellow, black, and white
  felt scraps
Pinking shears
Elmer's glue

10–12-inch long sharpened
  ⅛-inch dowel or other
  pointed small stick (a
  pencil will do)
Quilt batting
Fresh pineapple with
  many thick leaf fronds

Enlarge the above pattern so that each square equals one square inch. Then cut two of each pattern piece except the bottom front. Using pinking shears, cut out the red felt pieces and yellow beak pieces as shown. Pin or baste head pieces together, then stitch the beak side to where the stitching turns to form the beak. Stitching should form a ¼-inch seam on the outside of the turkey. Open the stitched-together head pieces to the side without the seam.

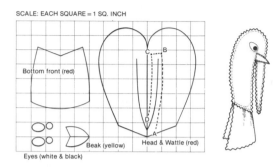

SCALE: EACH SQUARE = 1 SQ. INCH

Bottom front (red)

Beak (yellow)

Eyes (white & black)

Head & Wattle (red)

Pattern pieces for pineapple turkey.

Pineapple turkey centerpiece.

Pin or baste the bottom front piece—the bib—so that it overlaps the bottom of the head pieces, then stitch from each side up to ½ inch from the seam joining the head pieces. Turn head pieces back to seam side. Continue stitching head pieces together, starting at the beak corner, then stitching across to form head and down the middle of wattle pieces. Backstitch to secure at corner ends of seam. Begin stitching again at top of beak, then follow edge around head and down to bottom edge, leaving bottom open.

Stuff with batting until rounded and firm. Glue pointed tip of yellow beak pieces together, then glue to head with straight sides down and with rounded sides fit into and covering the seam. Glue white elliptical eye pieces in place, then glue black round eyeballs to finish the turkey's face. Poke dowel, sharpened side down, up into the batting, leaving three inches of the pointed end extended below batting.

To complete the turkey, push pointed dowel into the end of the fresh pineapple at angle shown so that the pineapple forms the turkey's body and the leaf fronds its tail.

Laundry Party

Housewives, executives, or singles—whoever you are—you will enjoy this unique party. Laundry day provides the theme, not necessarily the activity.

Begin by sending out your invitations on laundry receipts or detergent boxtops. Be sure to direct some of your guests to bring an iron along to "press" their dinners. Hang plastic garbage bags along a clothesline for guests to discard paper plates, cups, etc.

Menu

Ironed Pocket Sandwiches
Laundry Basket Fruit Salad
Garden Delight Kebabs (see p. 75)
Pressed Delight, served with
Homemade Ice Cream or Frozen Yogurt

Laundry party—with ironing board buffet and laundry-basket soda station.

Ironed Pocket Sandwiches

Cover a picnic table or several ironing boards with paper over several layers of newspaper for protection from spills. Set up several "ironing stations" with irons and at least six 12-by-18-inch sheets of aluminum foil for each guest to "cook" with. The number of stations will be determined by how many irons you can plug into your house or patio without blowing a fuse.

You and your guests should assemble the sandwich of your choice from suggestions below, or use any other melt-able fillings you can create.

Directions:

Cut pita bread to form pocket for fillings. (You can buy this bread at most grocery stores.) Fill with one of the following combinations:

- Monterey Jack cheese and canned green chili
- Corned beef, Swiss cheese and 1 tablespoon sauerkraut
- Precooked hamburger, diced onion, shredded cheese, and 1 tablespoon spaghetti or pizza sauce
- Mozzarella cheese, cooked hamburger and a tomato slice
- Tuna, chopped egg, chopped onion and green pepper, grated cheddar cheese

Butter pita bread on both sides. Place on 12-by-18-inch piece of aluminum foil. Cover sandwich with another foil piece the same size. Set hot iron on foil package for 30 seconds or until filling is warm and melted.

Ironing a pocket sandwich.

Laundry Basket Fruit Salad

This salad will highlight any party.

1 16-ounce can of cherries, pitted	½ pound miniature marshmallows
1 egg white	Juice of half lemon
1 pint whipping cream	½ pound slivered blanched almonds

Drain cherries. Whip the egg white and cream separately until each form soft peaks, and fold together. Add cherries, marshmallows, lemon juice and almonds. Toss together. Chill well. Serve in laundry basket filled with ice bowls (see p. 39).

Yield: **6–8 servings**

Luxury Fruit Liner

Decorative as well as truly tasty.

Large watermelon	Pineapple chunks
Grapes	Green apple chunks
Bananas, dipped in pineapple juice	Cantaloupe balls
	Pear chunks

Slice watermelon lengthwise. Using ice-cream scoop, hollow out 8 scoops of watermelon. Fill each scoop with fruit or fruit dip. Serve with toothpicks.

Luxury fruit liner with fruit dip.

Fruit Dip

2 egg yolks
⅓ cup sugar

1 6-ounce can frozen lemonade
  concentrate
1 cup heavy cream

Place water in bottom of double boiler and heat to boiling. In top of double boiler, beat egg yolks until lemon-colored, then stir in sugar and lemonade. Cook over boiling water, stirring constantly until thickened. Cool. Whip cream.

Add cooled egg mixture to whipped cream a little at a time. Whip until well mixed and smooth.

Pressed Delight

Ironing never tasted so good!

1 pound cake   6 chocolate bars

Slice pound cake into 12 slices. Place a chocolate bar between two slices of cake. Place candy sandwich in middle of a 12-by-18-inch sheet of aluminum foil. Cover with another sheet of foil. Hold hot iron so that it touches foil very lightly, for about 30 seconds or until chocolate begins to melt. Serve topped with homemade ice cream.

Yield: 6 servings

Pocket-Bread Pie

Another pocket-bread delight to "press" for dessert.

Cut pita or pocket bread to form pocket. Fill pocket with filling of your choice. Butter the pocket bread on both sides and place on 12-by-18-inch sheet of foil. Cover with another sheet of foil and press with hot iron for 30 seconds. Suggested fillings:

- ½ cup apple pie filling, 2 teaspoons butter, and ½ teaspoon ground cinnamon
- ½ cup cherry pie filling, 2 tablespoons crushed pineapple, 2 teaspoons butter

- ½ cup pie cherries and 3 tablespoons marshmallows (or marshmallow creme)
- ½ cup pie cherries and ¼ cup diced, cooked apples
- ½ cup blueberry pie filling, 2 teaspoons butter and dash cinnamon

Delicious Ice Cream

A sweet citrus treat.

6 oranges
6 lemons
6 cups sugar

1½ quarts milk
1½ quarts heavy cream

Place juice and pulp of fruits in blender and whip until relatively smooth. Add remaining ingredients. Freeze in ice cream freezer.

Yield: 6 quarts

Homemade Frozen Yogurt Delight

Frozen goodness.

10 cups lemon yogurt

⅔ cup frozen juice concentrate (orange or lemon)

Mix well, then freeze in ice-cream freezer.

Yield: 3 quarts

Flowerpot Party

For the first warm days in spring, what could be more appropriate than an outdoor flowerpot party?

Menu

Flower-Pink Dip with Chips and Vegetables
Hamburgers or Hot Dogs a la Flowerpot
Cheese Onions
Picnic Pudding Salad
Marinated Carrot Salad
Daffodil Frappé Punch
Ice Cream Flowerpot Pie

Flower-Pink Dip with Chips and Vegetables

As appetizers or as a delicious accompaniment to your hamburgers or hot dogs, serve this special dip in a hollowed-out red cabbage. Cut off top of cabbage and take out center. Line several small flowerpots with aluminum foil or plastic wrap, then stack a single vegetable in each pot: celery sticks in one, fresh cauliflower in another, carrot sticks in a third, etc. A larger lined flowerpot would make a good serving dish for potato chips.

2 8-ounce packages cream cheese	Pickled beet juice
	1 large red cabbage

Thin room-temperature cream cheese with beet juice until well blended to dip consistency. Serve dip in the cabbage "bowl" with beet and pickle slices, green pepper slivers, fresh cauliflower, celery and carrot sticks.

Yield: 8–10 servings

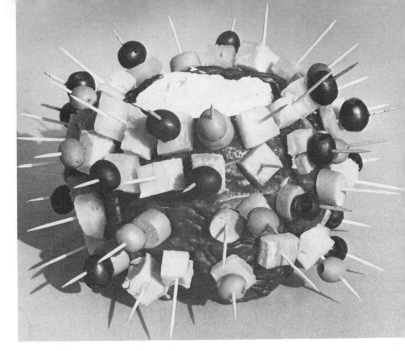

Flower-pink dip.

Hamburgers or Hot Dogs a la Flowerpot

You will need one flowerpot grill for each couple, following directions on p. 29. Request each couple to bring his own flowerpot and cookie-cooling rack. Then everyone could construct his own grill as the first activity of the party. Cook hot dogs or hamburgers on your grill.

Cooking hot dogs
on flowerpot grill.

Picnic Pudding Salad

Colorful as a flower garden.

1 20-ounce-can chunk
   pineapple, plus juice
1 16-ounce-can fruit
   cocktail, plus juice
1 11-ounce can mandarin
   oranges, drained

2 bananas, sliced
1 cup coconut
1 package instant lemon
   pudding mix (or any other
   flavor)

In medium-sized bowl, combine fruit and coconut. While stirring, sprinkle pudding mix over fruit and let stand 5 minutes. Add juice. Pudding will set in fruit juice.

Yield: 8 cups

Serve this tasty salad in a flowerpot, too. Line the pot well with foil or plastic wrap. Set a large plastic bag full of ice cubes in the bottom of the pot. Then nestle the bowl of salad into the ice cubes.

Marinated Carrot Salad

This salad offers a perfect complement to hamburgers.

5 cups (2 pounds) fresh carrots,
   cut in thick round chunks
1 large onion, sliced in thin
   rounds
1 large green pepper, chopped
1 10¾-ounce can tomato soup
⅓ cup salad oil
½ cup sugar

¾ cup vinegar
1 tablespoon prepared
   mustard
2 tablespoons Worcestershire
   sauce
1 teaspoon garlic powder
1 teaspoon salt

Cook carrots until almost done. Drain and cool. Mix with all other ingredients. Refrigerate 12 hours.

Yield: 10 servings

Cheese Onions

A spectacular way to serve onions.

24 small green onions
1 8-ounce package
   Philadelphia cream cheese

4 ounce grated cheese

Clean and trim onions so that they are about 6 inches long. Cream Philadelphia cream cheese until it can be spread with a knife. Spread cream cheese on bottom two inches of onions, then roll in grated cheese.

Daffodil Frappé Punch

Flower-pretty and tasty, too.

6 cups water
3 cups sugar
1 3 oz. package lemon Jello
Juice of 3 lemons
Juice of 3 oranges

1½ cups pineapple juice
1 quart ginger ale
3 bananas, blended
12 daffodils in straws, for
   garnish

Heat water and sugar until sugar dissolves. Add Jello and stir until dissolved. When cool, add lemon, orange, and pineapple juices. Freeze in trays. One hour before using, remove mixture from freezer. Mix equal amounts of fruit mixture and ginger ale, and stir two to three tablespoons banana into each glass. Slip daffodil over each straw (at least 3 inches down so flower stands up). Serve with daffodil-straw sticking up from drink in tumbler "flowerpot."

Yield: 12 servings.

Ice Cream Flowerpot Pie

This unique recipe
will top off your party.

8 flat-bottomed paper cups
1 quart chocolate ice cream
24 Oreo cookies
8 plastic spoons
8 flowers, artificial or real, for
  garnish

Ice cream flowerpot pie.

To "plant" your ice-cream flower garden, fill a paper cup to within a half-inch of the top with chocolate ice cream. Remove the frosting centers from Oreos (each "flowerpot" takes about 3 cookies) and place the cookies in a plastic bag. Crush cookies with a rolling pin. Sprinkle the crushed cookies over the chocolate ice cream. Place the dessert in the freezer until serving time. (If you want to use real flowerpots, line them first with aluminum foil.) When you are ready to serve the treat, stick plastic spoons with fresh or artificial flowers attached to the handles upright in the ice cream.

Yield: 8 servings

Flower Pattern

To make an attractive paper flower for your flowerpot pie, cut 2 sets of petals from two 5-inch squares of brightly colored construction paper, or felt. Paste together so they fit over the spoon handle.

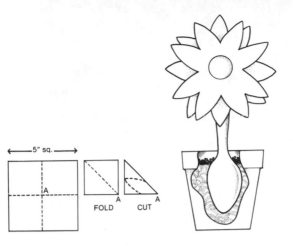

Sample flower pattern to be cut from the 5-inch squares of construction paper or felt.

Especially for Children

Children love parties, whether they are celebrating a birthday, a special holiday, or any old day. Here's an outdoor menu to set any child jumping for joy:

Menu

Monster Dogs
Marshmallow Fruit Faces
Animal Salad
Crazy Cones, Orange Supreme Floats, or Snowball Animals

Monster Dogs

Monster Dogs are not only fun and creative, but they are great to eat too. Help the children slice the frankfurters so that each has several long and short cuts in them. Grill the franks on your outdoor grill until sizzling. As the franks cook, they will curl to form animal monsters. Serve on hot-dog or hamburger buns depending on the shape of the animal you make. You will need plenty of franks, because each child will probably want to make more than one.

Monster dogs.

Animal salad.

Marshmallow Fruit Faces

Children from three to eighty-three will love this.

1 cup fruit cocktail, drained
1 cup sour cream
1 cup pineapple chunks
1 cup coconut flakes

1 cup miniature
   marshmallows
Sugar to taste
Maraschino cherries (for color)
1 orange, sectioned

Toss first six ingredients together and let stand overnight in refrigerator or until marshmallows lose their identity. Serve in scoops. Make a face on each scoop by arranging an orange section for a mouth and maraschino cherry halves for eyes.

Yield: 8–12 servings

Animal Salad

"Cookies" packed with nutrition.

1 package each American and   Lettuce
  Swiss cheese slices   Sweet or dill pickle slices

Cut each cheese slice in animal shapes using sharp-edged cookie cutters. Arrange each cheese "animal" on top of a leaf of lettuce and a pickle slice. Garnish with olives.

Crazy Cones

This dessert is everybody's favorite.

Use flat-bottomed ice-cream cones and fill with any of the different fillings suggested below. Make the fillings ahead of time and refrigerate. Spoon into cones just before serving. (Cones will become soggy if they sit too long with filling inside.) You might want to make more than one filling and let the children choose the one they want. The children will love these new creations and will make less mess eating their dessert in a cone. Here are some suggested fillings:

Pudding Cones

4 to 6 flat-bottomed cones   1 cup heavy cream whipped
1 3-ounce package pudding   ⅓ cup each miniature
  and pie filling (chocolate is   marshmallows and banana
  a good bet)   slices (optional)
1¾ cups milk

Make pudding according to package directions, using 1¾ cups milk instead of 2 cups. Blend in 1 cup whipped cream. If desired add bananas and miniature marshmallows.

Yield: 4–6 servings, depending on size of cone

Fruit Yummy Cones

6 to 8 flat-bottomed cones
1 cup heavy cream, whipped

1 16-ounce can fruit cocktail
or 2 cups fresh fruit or 2 cups
frozen raspberries or
strawberries, thawed
½ cup each miniature
marshmallows and sliced
bananas (optional)

Combine 1 cup of whipped cream with fruit choice. If desired, add bananas and colored miniature marshmallows. Chill until ready to use.

Yield: 6–8 servings

Cherry-Cheese Cones

6 to 8 flat-bottomed cones
1 8-ounce package cream
cheese

1 16-ounce can cherry-pie
filling

Soften cream cheese at room temperature. Place into a bowl and stir until creamy smooth. With a knife or spatula, spread the cream cheese around the inside of the cones about ¼-inch thick. Fill cones with cherry pie filling and dot the top with cream cheese.

Yield: 6–8 servings

Cakey Cones

8–10 flat-bottomed cones

Variation 1: 1 7-ounce package muffin mix
1 16-ounce can pie filling

Variation 2: 1 one-layer cake mix
1 3-ounce package pudding and pie filling
1½ cups milk

Prepare muffin mix according to package directions. Put one tablespoon of batter in bottom of each cone. Add one tablespoon of canned pie filling (for example, use Apple Cinnamon Muffin mix with apple pie filling). Then add two more tablespoons batter. Set on baking sheet in muffin tin and bake at 425° F. for about 15 to 20 minutes.

Yield: 6 servings

If you substitute cake mix for muffin mix and use prepared pudding and pie filling instead of canned pie filling, bake at 350 degrees F. for 15 to 20 minutes, or until done. Frost with favorite frosting.

Yield: 8–10 servings

Ice Cream Puff Cones

6 to 8 flat-bottomed cones   2 cups self-rising flour
1 pint ice cream, favorite flavor

Mix ice cream and flour together, then fill cones ⅔ full with batter. Place cones in muffin tins and bake at 350 degrees F. for 15 to 20 minutes, or until done.

Yield: 6–8 servings

Orange Supreme Float

Hot summer days call for cool, refreshing drinks.

12 large oranges   1 32-ounce bottle orange soda
1 pint orange sherbet

Cut the top quarter off each orange. With a grapefruit or paring knife, cut around the inside of the orange as you

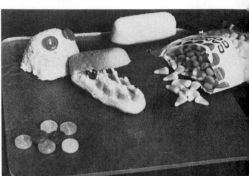

Orange supreme float.   Snow-ball animals.

would a grapefruit. Spoon out and remove the orange pulp, place it in a container, and store pulp in the refrigerator to use for morning juice. When ready to serve, nestle a small scoop of orange sherbet into an orange shell, then pour orange soda over the top. Serve with a straw. You will be amazed at how the flavors blend to create a novel dessert. (Fresh orange juice can be made from the orange pulp in your blender.)

Yield: 12 servings

Snowball Animals

You can be eating caterpillars, ladybugs, worms, turtles, and other outdoor beasts if you use a little ingenuity. When it's time to serve refreshments, you can use Snow-Balls, Twinkies, doughnuts and other goodies to design an entire menagerie. For example, for an alligator, use a Snow-Ball for the head, a Twinkie sliced lengthwise (to about one inch from the end) for the jaws, Lifesavers or other candies for the eyes and tongue, and two matchsticks with the tips burned for teeth.

Have a monster-designing contest, using the same materials. You and your children will come up with an entirely new cast of scary creatures that will demand eradication—by eating.

184

Party Planning Guide

Type of Party _____

Date _____ Time _____

Guest List

Name   Phone

Menu

RECIPES

Advance Schedule

Two or Three Weeks Ahead
_____Pick a theme.
_____Make and send invitations.
_____Plan menu.
_____Plan activities.

Several Days Ahead
_____Shop (groceries, table supplies, charcoal briquets and starter fluid).
_____Prepare and freeze as much as possible in advance.
_____Check outdoor equipment (grill, wood supply, and utensils).
_____Plan lighting for patio.
_____Stock up on insecticides if insects are a problem.

The Day Before
_____Prepare yard (mow lawn, weed, etc.).
_____Arrange tables and settings.
_____Shop for fresh food items.
_____Arrange lighting.

Day of Party

Suggested List
This is a list of things to jab your memory, but not all are necessary for each party. Move items from this list onto your "Actual Plan"—on the next page.

Shop for last-minute items, perishables.
Last-minute cleaning.

Arrange centerpieces.
Set tables.
Organize equipment for games, activities.
Prepare: Drink
          Salad(s)
          Dessert
          Bread
          Entrée
          Vegetable
          Hors d'oeuvres
Plan cleanup.
Arrange background music.
Prepare fire.

Actual

Start filling in schedule as needed:

10:00 A.M._____

11:00 A.M._____

 4:00 P.M._____

 4:30 P.M._____

 5:00 P.M._____

 5:30 P.M._____

 6:00 P.M._____

 6:30 P.M._____

 7:00 P.M. Pre-party activities for early arrivals
 7:30 P.M. Party begins
Cleanup—garbage cans or plastic garbage bag on clothes-line.

Shopping Organizer

Fresh fruit and vegetables	Dairy products	Meat products
Canned goods	Paper supplies	Frozen foods
Junk foods	Breads	Miscellaneous

Index